BY WORSHIPING IN SPIRIT AND IN TRUTH

Becoming a Holy Spirit-Led, Manifest Child of God
Who Ignites Unstoppable, Joyful, Revival Fires
of Supernatural Power

JOHN W. NICHOLS

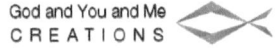

Becoming Supernatural by Worshiping in Spirit and in Truth:
Becoming a Holy Spirit-Led, Manifest Child of God,
Who Ignites Unstoppable, Joyful, Revival Fires of Supernatural Power
Copyright © 2024 by John W. Nichols.
All rights reserved. Printed in the United States of America. No part of this book may be used or reproduced in any manner whatsoever without written permission except in the case of brief quotations embodied in critical articles or reviews.
Published in Shenandoah, Texas, by God and You and Me CREATIONS.
For information contact: John@GodAndYouAndMe.com

Edited by Joanne Hillman, www.JoanneHillman.com
Cover design and book formatting by John Nichols
www.GodAndYouAndMe.com/BookHelp

Cover Photo, Brooklyn Font, and Breathine Font downloaded from CreativeFabrica.com with permission by the Subscription License

Scripture quotations marked AMP are taken from the Amplified® Bible, Copyright © 2015 by The Lockman Foundation. Used by permission. www.Lockman.org

Scripture quotations marked AMPC are taken from the Amplified® Bible, Copyright © 1954, 1958, 1962, 1964, 1965, 1987 by The Lockman Foundation. Used by permission. www.Lockman.org

Scripture quotations marked NASB are taken from the NEW AMERICAN STANDARD BIBLE®, Copyright © 1960,1962,1963,1968,1971,1972,1973,1975,1977,1995 by The Lockman Foundation. Used by permission.

Scripture quotations marked NKJV are taken from the New King James Version®. Copyright © 1982 by Thomas Nelson. Used by permission. All rights reserved.

Scripture quotations marked NLT are taken from the Holy Bible, New Living Translation, copyright © 1996, 2004, 2015 by Tyndale House Foundation. Used by permission of Tyndale House Publishers, Inc., Carol Stream, Illinois 60188. All rights reserved.

Scripture quotations marked TPT are from The Passion Translation®. Copyright © 2017, 2018 by Passion & Fire Ministries, Inc. Used by permission. All rights reserved. ThePassionTranslation.com.

Translations of Hebrew and Greek words taken from Strong's Exhaustive Concordance, Copyright © 1890 by James Strong, S.T.D., LL.D. Public Domain.

Print Edition September 2024 ISBN: 978-1-7328093-4-5
Epub Edition September 2024 ISBN: 979-8-3304-0040-9
Kindle Edition September 2024 ASIN: B0DFWLXNH6
10 9 8 7 6 5 4 3 2 1

For the Church,
the body and the bride of Christ.

Contents

Introduction 1

Ch. 1: Falling in Love with the God of the Bible, and Not Religion 11

Ch. 2: Never Stop Praying 21

Ch. 3: Hearing God and Knowing His Will 33

Ch. 4: God's Glorious Word 45

Ch. 5: Being Submerged in His Spirit 57

Ch. 6: The Secret Place of Meeting with God 71

Ch. 7: Foundations of Reality from the Old Testament 81

Ch. 8: Supernatural Scripture and Our Destiny 109

Ch. 9: The Power of Praise and His Presence 127

Ch. 10: Practically Applying the Word 135

Ch. 11: Following the Spirit of Truth 145

Additional Notes 157

Free Stuff!...161

About theAuthor..163

Introduction

For those who live according to the flesh set their minds on the things of the flesh, but those who live according to the Spirit, the things of the Spirit. For to be carnally minded is death, but to be spiritually minded is life and peace.

Romans 8:5-6 NKJV

I'M SO GLAD THAT you are continuing with me in the second book of the Revival Fire-Starters series! I'm excited for what God is doing in you and through you, and I am praying over you as you read the words in this book. We are going to be talking about Becoming Supernatural by Worshiping in Spirit and in Truth. Each of these words is important.

Becoming

Most people spend their time focused on their physical

life and the natural world. They look at the people around them, and if they judge beyond the external, it is only as deep as someone's thoughts, emotions, habits, and personality. But we need to recognize that everyone and everything around us is more than natural. There is something above, encompassing the natural—something supernatural.

In the last book, I briefly mentioned how we are body, soul, and spirit. And our spirit comes to life at salvation. I also wrote that by faith we know that there are things which exist that we cannot see (Hebrews 11:1). And how Jesus lived a supernatural life. The fact that we are supposed to follow in His footsteps was a topic delved into a bit more. In this book we're going to dive deeper into the supernatural as we consider spiritual truths.

My goal is that you would become something. Even if I give you no new information, I hope that you start one way and end up changed for the better. As you embrace ideas about the spiritual realm and they are realized, I pray you become supernatural. That your experience and personification supersede the ways of this world, and expand into God's heavenly ways and kingdom.

Supernatural

The truth is the supernatural realm or the spiritual

realm is just as real, if not more real, than the natural realm. That means we need to shift our thinking. We need our minds to be changed, to be transformed, to become something different. We need to realize that our life and the things we should value are essentially above nature. At the same time as being grounded on this earth, we are above. Supernatural. What we can explain, quantify, and experience with our five physical senses is not all there is to existence.

> *Asked by the Pharisees when the kingdom of God would come, He replied to them by saying, The kingdom of God does not come with signs to be observed or with visible display, Nor will people say, Look! Here [it is]! or, See, [it is] there! For behold, the kingdom of God is within you [in your hearts] and among you [surrounding you].*
> Luke 17:20-21 AMPC

The kingdom of God is in your midst. It's at hand! And this kingdom is a supernatural kingdom. It's a kingdom that weaves in and encompasses, envelopes, and soaks in everything natural, even all lesser kingdoms. Its laws are above. And yet they impact and work with natural laws and our physical experience—therefore valuing them. These realities work together and affect one another.

Even when we don't recognize it, the supernatural—the spiritual dimension—truly exists and is taking place in conjunction with normal life. Many will solely look at the natural and think that's all there is to experience. But the truth is, these people are affecting things in the supernatural, and things are affecting them from the supernatural.

By Worshiping

The focus and method of each individual's worship will transform that person's life. And it will also affect the spiritual realm. What we look at in awe and adoration is literally capable of changing us. And because God made us in His image to create, our worship is spiritually charged and powerful. Anyone practicing the occult will tell you beyond the shadow of a doubt that their witchcraft and sacrifices make real impacts on both the natural and spiritual realms.

This is one reason it's imperative that we worship the One True and Living God. We become supernatural as we worship Him who preceded and created nature. And our genuine, sacrificial love changes us to look more like Our Father in Heaven. Not only that, but any born-again believer who has spent a significant amount of time praying can testify that it effects the natural and spiritual realms.

So we must worship, but especially in spirit and in truth. As Jesus said, "the hour is coming, and now is, when the true worshipers will worship the Father in spirit and truth; for the Father is seeking such to worship Him. God is Spirit, and those who worship Him must worship in spirit and truth (John 4:23-24 NKJV)."

In Spirit

In the last book we recognized how the Pharisees had in their own traditions perfected religion to keep them in good standing with God, and yet they were children of wrath. They could not see what God was doing in front of their very eyes. Even though they had a form of the truth, righteousness, and godliness—they didn't have the Spirit.

> *There was a man named Nicodemus, a Jewish religious leader who was a Pharisee. After dark one evening, he came to speak with Jesus. "Rabbi," he said, "we all know that God has sent you to teach us. Your miraculous signs are evidence that God is with you."*
>
> *Jesus replied, "I tell you the truth, unless you are born again, you cannot see the Kingdom of God."*
>
> *"What do you mean?" exclaimed Nicodemus. "How can an old man go back into his mother's*

womb and be born again?"

Jesus replied, "I assure you, no one can enter the Kingdom of God without being born of water and the Spirit. Humans can reproduce only human life, but the Holy Spirit gives birth to spiritual life. So don't be surprised when I say, 'You must be born again.' The wind blows wherever it wants. Just as you can hear the wind but can't tell where it comes from or where it is going, so you can't explain how people are born of the Spirit."

"How are these things possible?" Nicodemus asked.

Jesus replied, "You are a respected Jewish teacher, and yet you don't understand these things? I assure you, we tell you what we know and have seen, and yet you won't believe our testimony. But if you don't believe me when I tell you about earthly things, how can you possibly believe if I tell you about heavenly things?

John 3:1-12 NLT

Despite all his religious training, Nicodemus needed the Spirit to truly understand heavenly things. Likewise, we must worship in the Spirit. The Holy Spirit is the Spirit of truth and discloses all things the Father has (John 16:13-

15). Not many theologians would like to admit that, according to scripture, you don't even need a teacher, because His anointing abides in you and teaches you all things (1 John 2:27)!

And in Truth

So we must recognize that the Holy Spirit will lead us into the truth and...

> *All scripture is inspired by God and beneficial for teaching, for rebuke, for correction, for training in righteousness; so that the man or woman of God may be fully capable, equipped for every good work.*
> 2 Timothy 3:16-17 NASB

If all scripture is God-breathed, it is the truth. God's Word, the Bible, will teach, rebuke, correct, and train us. The Holy Spirit will use the Bible to help us become able and equipped for what He wants to do through us. So in this book we'll be talking a lot about the Bible, how to practically take it in, understand it, and apply it. And we are going to be talking a lot about the Spirit of God. How to practically connect with His Spirit, receive from His Spirit, and walk in the things of the Spirit.

When you combine these things along with

understanding and operating in true God-designed worship, then I promise you are going to become supernatural. This is the next step along the path of becoming a Holy Spirit-led, manifest child of God, who ignites unstoppable, joyful, revival fires of supernatural power!

The Workbook and Free Downloads Will Help Set You Ablaze!

You'll get the most out of this book by using the accompanying workbook. The print edition is currently available only on Amazon, and will include a link inside to download the PDF version for free. If you do not have Amazon in your area, you can email me and I will send you the PDF of the workbook (contact information in the About the Author section). This workbook includes thought provoking questions, journaling prompts, and practical next steps suggestions. Scan here to get it:

GodAndYouAndMe.com/recommends/becoming-supernatural-workbook/

Get These Free Resources Together

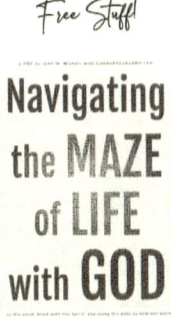

Simple Steps to Hearing God — Walk with God, Change the World — Revolutionize Your Quiet Time

Subscribe at: GodAndYouAndMe.com/becoming-supernatural-free-stuff

- *God is Trying to Tell You Something.* An audio teaching in MP3 format, focused on the key to hearing God, common ways God speaks, and practical steps to hear Him today.
- *7 Keys to a Successful Time of Devotion to God.* A PDF with steps to include in your quiet time.
- *Navigating the Maze of Life with God.* A 60-page PDF about giving your life to God, being filled with the Holy Spirit, and walking in the power of the Holy Spirit to live the life God intended you to live.
- Additional content only available to subscribers on GodAndYouAndMe.com. You can unsubscribe at any time and I promise not to

spam you.

Get these free resources here (Most phones are capable of using the camera app to follow this link. Simply open the camera on your phone and point it at the page):

GodAndYouAndMe.com/becoming-supernatural-free-stuff

Chapter 1

Falling in Love with the God of the Bible, and Not Religion

I have longed for You with the passion of my heart; don't let me stray from Your directions! I consider Your Word to be my greatest treasure, and I treasure it in my heart to keep me from committing sin's treason against You. My wonderful God, You are to be praised above all; teach me the power of Your decrees!

Psalm 119:10-12 TPT

Becoming Supernatural

Treasuring Scripture

AROUND THE TIME I surrendered my life to Jesus, I developed an unquenchable thirst for scripture. God had literally spoken to me that if I wanted to know Him, I needed to know His Word. His still small voice imparted faith in the Holy Bible as the Word of God, and that faith sparked a fire that burned in my heart for years. During all my free time, I was reading the Word, and before I knew it, I was attending three Bible studies, Sunday School, and church every week.

One day I was somehow roped into facilitating a Bible study when I definitely had no business leading anyone. It was just me and another guy that day, and it's funny because I probably was not even ahead of him in my walk with God. But he was surprised by the way I talked about the Bible. I was excited about the passage we had read, imagining the possibilities of the Biblical figure's perspective. This young Christian was inspired that I was inspired. He said half in disbelief, half in awe, "You talk about these people like they're real."

In a way I was shocked. At the hint of his disbelief, yes, but also because I had taken for granted the gift I had been given of faith in God's Word. Of course these were real people, so why wouldn't I think of them that way? I had fallen in love with the Bible and the flawed heroes on its pages. More than that, as my wrong ideas about God were being stripped away by His Word, I was falling more and more in love with the Author of the Bible.

I loved the One who spoke everything into existence. The One whose love never ceases and His mercies are new every morning. The One whose anger over a nation's unfaithfulness was eased by one friend humbling himself in prayer. The One who miraculously worked in the lives of individuals and kingdoms to correct, rescue, guide, and protect. The One who stripped Himself of His rightful omnipotence, omniscience, and omnipresence to become like His creation and save the world.

Breaking All the Boxes and Escaping Religion

Despite my genuine love for God, and how His Word was helping me to come out of wrong ideas and bad teaching I had received, at some point the spirit of religion secretly hopped on for a ride. Though I didn't recognize it for years and it caused me to struggle in receiving the things of the Spirit, God again spoke and broke Himself out of a major box I had put Him in. I'll go into more detail on this in Chapter 5. For now, my focus is to help you stay in your first love of God, and not religion.

As I continued walking with Jesus, I experienced many different denominations and variations in Christian

Becoming Supernatural

teachings. And when I became involved in a church that exalted theology and "sound doctrine," it was like that little demon of religion was injected with growth hormones. I became so engrossed in theology that every verse of the Bible I read, and every prayer I prayed, became jaded with man's attempt to explain God. Theology isn't necessarily wrong in itself, but the teaching I was studying was founded on some wrong definitions of certain words and many wrong ideas about God.

We talked in the first book about how God saved us for relationship, not religion. And we need to touch on it again because a major focus of this book is the Bible. Which sounds funny to say, as I've already shared my deep love for the Bible (which I still carry). We desperately need the Bible. We would do good to treasure it as the Psalmist of 119. The Bible is undoubtedly perfect and is God's Word. And I have to be thankful for the foundation I had in the Bible because I have seen what happens to people without it. But as we study the Bible, we must not lose track of the living Author of the Bible, who is still active today and in whom we also live and move and have our being (Acts 17:28).

As you testify of your experiences with this living God, some might say it's the work of demons, or there is no precedence in scripture for what you describe (as the religious people love to say these days). You can remind them that the people who were writing the Bible were experiencing things with God that no one had ever experienced before. In other words, there was not precedence in scripture, for the things that happened in scripture! Doesn't God still move, or did He become a mute idol upon the canonization of the Holy Bible? And wasn't Jesus also accused of operating under the influence of demons (Matthew 2:22-29)?

Don't get me wrong, I love looking at God's Word for precedence. But more to expand my little brain on what's possible for me to experience, than to shut someone down who is genuinely seeking God. The fact of the matter is, as we look at the Bible with a theologian's perspective, as one who studies God, it is a slippery slope of becoming like the Pharisees and today's practitioners of theology who for some reason keep attributing the works of God to demons.

Let's face it, droves of people are being led into a "Christian" belief system that is carnal, or at best soulish. They shy away from the power and mystery of the supernatural, and anything outside their ability to understand or perform with human knowledge, strength, and discipline. They stray from the living God to one that can be boxed up and explained, all the while touting their sound doctrine. We don't want that. We want to stay close, in relationship. Falling more in love with God as we fall in love with His Word.

> [Jesus] answered and said to [the Pharisees and scribes], "Well did Isaiah prophesy of you hypocrites, as it is written:
>
>> 'This people honors Me with their lips,
>> But their heart is far from Me.
>> And in vain they worship Me,
>> Teaching as doctrines the commandments of men.'"
>
> ... He said to them, "All too well you reject the commandment of God, that you may keep your tradition... making the word of God of no effect through your tradition which you have handed down."
>
> Mark 7:6-7, 9, 13a NKJV
> (read also Matthew 23:11-15)

A Heart Near to God

Remain in love with the God of the Bible, the One who was alive before, during, and after the Inspired Word was written. He is the Author of your faith, who has written a beautiful story for you to join in. I'm sorry to tell you this, but you can't read all of your story in the Bible and no seminary can teach you it. In fact, they may say your story's written in stone, so just go with the flow, but I'm telling you that's a doctrine of devils meant to kill your fruit on the vine. You'll only learn what God's written for you to do, and be who He created you to be, by keeping your heart close to Him.

Saul (who later became Paul) thought he was doing God's work, persecuting born again believers in the newly formed Church. Meanwhile God was trying to get his attention and transform him. When Jesus humbled Saul with a blinding light, and he repented, it was a beautiful thing (Acts 26:1-20). Likewise, we must allow any wrong ideas in us to be exposed and made new by God's light. The Holy Spirit has showed me many things that at first I was opposed to because I thought they weren't Biblical. Then He showed me through scripture how I was wrong, that I had a bad interpretation of His Word because of someone's theology that I had received. When I realized that God was trying to move in my life and I was fighting against Him, I quickly repented.

God wants to speak into your life. Both through the Bible and through His Spirit. We're going to talk a lot about these things, and both are very good. The Bible must be the basis of your understanding of truth, your belief system, and your world-view. But He also wants to speak things to you that are not in the Bible. Although what He truly speaks will not be contrary to His written Word, it can be hard to separate learned doctrine from actual truth. So you must be flexible and allow Him to break any boxes which man's tradition and religion have put you in. If you always keep your heart near to God, stoking the fire of your love for Him who is the Author of the Bible, you will be in a good place.

Our amazing God shows us in the Bible that spiritual realities should not be understood as separate from the natural. Both Old and New Testament stories reveal these realms exist simultaneously and work together. Nothing has changed, and what we see happening in "normal" life continues to have direct correlations with hidden spiritual motivators. This can be easily recognized by looking at the depravity in the world and it's demonic roots. But we can use our natural tongue and words to actually effect and change those situations, even commanding demons to leave in the name of Jesus. We can lay our physical hand on a person who is sick and something spiritual happens as they begin to recover. As a person is transformed in the inner-man, their external life begins to radically change for the better. We must not only become supernatural, but realize we already are.

Prayer

I love You, God, and I treasure everything You say. Both the scriptures and Your Spirit speaking to me. I ask for a gift of deeper faith that the Bible is Your inspired Word, and for discernment and faith in recognizing Your true voice. As I read the Bible, please help me have profound revelation and help me to fall more in love with You, God. Please protect my heart from becoming like the scribes and the Pharisees who knew Your Word and whose arguments sounded good from the outside, but their hearts were far from You. Please rescue me if I have fallen into any trap of religion, received skewed theology, or my beliefs have limited Your work in my life. I ask for Your light to shine in me, expose any wrong way, and transform me. Most of all draw my heart ever closer to You, the Author and finisher of my faith. In Jesus's name, I pray. Amen.

Don't Forget!

If you haven't already, you can purchase the accompanying workbook, which will help you think deeper about these topics and apply the Biblical truths, especially if you step out in faith and follow the recommended Action Items. I created it as another tool for you to become a Holy Spirit-led, manifest child of God, who ignites unstoppable, joyful, revival fires of supernatural power!

Becoming Supernatural

Perfect-bound print edition available only on Amazon (includes a link to download the PDF version for free): GodAndYouAndMe.com/recommends/becoming-supernatural-workbook

Most phones are capable of using the camera app to follow this link. Simply open the camera on your phone and point it at the page. If you do not have Amazon in your area, you can contact me using the About the Author section, and I will send you a PDF of the workbook.

Be sure to also to get the free resources here: GodAndYouAndMe.com/becoming-supernatural-free-stuff

Chapter 2

Never Stop Praying

Rejoice always, pray without ceasing, in everything give thanks; for this is the will of God in Christ Jesus for you.
Do not quench the Spirit. Do not despise prophecies. Test all things; hold fast what is good. Abstain from every form of evil.

1 Thessalonians 5:16-22
NKJV

What Prayer Really Is

AS WE SEEK TO worship God in spirit and in truth, one of our main means of worshiping is prayer. We should really understand prayer before getting into any methods, like praying without ceasing, praying in the

Spirit, or praying the Word of God (which are all wonderful and practical tools). We need to know that if we boil down prayer to the simplest definition, it is talking with God.

Prayer is communicating with the Father, Son, and Holy Spirit. We shouldn't limit it to ideas such as asking God for something, praying for someone else, or telling Him how good He is. All these things happen in prayer, but ultimately, we should think of it as simply the conversational aspect of fellowshipping with Him. Because we love Jesus, we know our Heavenly Father takes good care of us, and His Spirit is always with us, it should be normal for us to talk with Him—at all times—about everything.

Some will tell you it's wrong to ask God for blessings, or you shouldn't pray for someone to be healed, or not to fight against demons. They think poverty, sickness, and the work of the devil are God's will. But a deep relationship with God will lead to conversing with Him about *everything*. It's natural to ask for help and favor. It's natural to talk with Him about your loved ones who need healing. It's natural to seek Him when things are coming against you.

As you pray, you show that you recognize, value, and live by truths that are deeper and beyond the natural. Your prayer life reveals how much you believe the things of the spirit are real. Your faith-filled stand against giving up and accepting whatever comes in this life, will bring heavenly realities to earth. You will overcome the veil of the enemies lies and the fog of war, by living as if there is a truth that is deeper than your natural perceptions. This spiritual reality includes not only the Godhead of the Trinity, heavenly realms and creatures, the angelic, and the demonic; but also your own spirit and spiritual weapons—which are mighty through God to the pulling down of strongholds (2 Corinthians 10:3-6)!

By the way, this kind of constant dialog with God throughout your day, no matter what is going on around you, and living as though the supernatural is real is how you never stop praying. The verses above also say to rejoice always and give thanks in everything. You will do these things more and more, as you continue to receive greater revelation of who God is, who you are, and His promises to work everything out for your good.

When you live this way, you will become supernatural by reason of your intimacy with Jesus and how your prayer-life effects the world around you. He will give you wisdom and revelation. As you confide in Him and He in you, you will know things by the Spirit that you couldn't know in the natural. Your abiding in Him will not only cause you to bear fruit, but it will also equate to friendship with Him, and He will make known to you all things that He hears from the Father (John 15:1-15).

The Word Teaches Us How to Pray

The Bible is our foundation, and it even teaches us how to pray. Scripture is chock-full of prayer examples for us to model. For instance, we can see how Jesus communicated with the Father, and how He often sought Him in solitude (Luke 5:16, Matthew 6:6-7, Luke 4:1-2). There's a passage where Jesus gives His disciples a sort of prayer template (Matthew 6:9-13). The way people approached Jesus and were commended for their tenacity and faith reveals something about prayer. And Jesus's parables often give insights about prayer as well.

We find many examples of how people talked with God as we look at lives in the Old Testament, people like Job, Abraham, Moses, King David, and the prophets to name a few. They met with God face to face, asking Him to provide for their needs, turning away from their sins in repentance, humbling themselves and bowing before Him, asking Him to save and deliver, lifting their hands in worship and praising Him, joining in with angels crying out, "Holy!" All of these and so many more are ways that that people prayed in the Bible.

Just remember as you read these examples in the Bible (especially the Old Testament), it is a transcript of that person's perspective and not always the perfect model of how you should pray, believe, speak, or act. Because of the new covenant afforded by Jesus's blood, we are in a different position than these Old Testament believers. So, a good understanding of the whole story of scripture will help you to pray from the standing that people like Paul prayed—from a position of being seated with Christ in heavenly places. Still the Psalms show us so much about prayer.

Praying in the Spirit helps us to pray rightly even though we don't understand or have the words (see 1 Corinthians 14, and we'll discuss this more later). Praying scripture, however, helps us to pray rightly with our understanding engaged, even when we don't have the words. We could devote a whole chapter to the method of praying scripture. But to put it simply, if you are ever at a loss for words, it's hard to go wrong with speaking the words of the Bible to God, and even adjusting them to fit your circumstance. Below is an example of how you can turn the Bible into prayer, based on Hebrews 5:11-14 (see Amplified Classic Version for original wording).

> *Holy Spirit, please help me to receive the deep things of God. That my spiritual hearing would be sharpened, and I would be zealous in spiritual insight. Help me graduate to being able to teach others. That I could receive and*

teach upon the foundations of faith and God's Word. Help me to grow up from only drinking milk and that I would be able to consume solid spiritual food. I desire to experience and to practice the doctrine of righteousness. I want to conform to Your divine will in purpose, thought, and action. I want to grow up from a mere infant, so I can digest solid spiritual food like a full-grown man. I will train my spiritual senses and mental faculties by practice in order to discriminate and distinguish between what is morally good and noble, and what is evil and contrary either to divine or human law. Thank you, Lord, for helping me to grow into this and walk this out. In Jesus's name, amen!

There are also many prayers already sprinkled throughout the New Testament which can be used. Some refer to them as apostolic prayers and/or benedictions. These can be easily changed to apply to yourself, your family, or others. Here's a good list that I pray nearly every day:

- Romans 11:33-36
- Romans 15:13
- 2 Corinthians 2:14–16

- Ephesians 1:3-8
- Ephesians 1:17-23
- Ephesians 3:14-21
- Ephesians 6:19–20
- Philippians 1:3–6
- Philippians 1:9-11
- Colossians 1:9-14
- 2 Thessalonians 1:11-12
- 2 Thessalonians 3:1-3
- See if you can find more as you read the Bible!

Most importantly, remember that prayer is communication with God, and it is two ways. Do not allow methods of prayer, or even praying verses of the Bible, to replace spontaneous, authentic, and unrehearsed conversations with the Lord. People not only talked with God in the Bible, but they heard Him and received from Him through visions and experiences both in the natural and heavenly realms. We are going to look at how to practically hear Him in the next chapter, and we'll dive more into spiritual visions and experiences later in the series.

Parts of Ministry that are Actually Not Prayer

You never see Jesus and His disciples minister healing

to people or cast out demons by talking with God (see examples including Luke 13:11-13, Mark 5:2-13, and Acts 3:1-16). For some reason most people do not copy the way this ministry has been modeled for us in scripture. Instead, even pastors and chaplains ask God to do it, and assume whatever happens is His will.

But that's not what we see Jesus or His apostles do. We might not even consider it prayer. We can pray (talk with God) at the same time, or we can pray before or after. But there's something different happening when laying hands on someone, commanding healing. And something entirely different when ministering deliverance by commanding evil spirits to leave in the name of Jesus.

Now when we talk about Jesus healing a person's heart, where there's brokenness, that certainly includes prayer. But there's also ministry to the person's body, soul, and spirit. Speaking to that person and even to their natural and supernatural parts. Obviously, the coaching and counseling involved is not prayer, but it is as they speak to Jesus and invite Him in, or the minister listens to Jesus and speaks what He is saying. As well as helping people to pray and connect with God in order to receive from Him.

As we speak things in faith, prophesy the promises of God, and command things like the weather to get in line, it's also not prayer. All of these things are examples of acting in accordance with who God says we are (which we discussed at length in the first book). When Jesus did these things, He was in communion with His Father and led by the Holy Spirit, but instead of talking to God, He spoke to the thing that needed to be changed. As always, He is our ultimate example and who we should try to model.

Communion with God

A verse that is often quoted during evangelistic messages is Revelation 3:20 when Jesus says, "Behold, I stand at the door and knock; if anyone hears My voice and opens the door, I will come in to him and will dine with him, and he with Me (NLT)." It's wonderful how Jesus wants to commune with us in this way—as a friend. Notice, in this verse He is not inviting you into a grand banqueting hall in His Father's heavenly cathedral. But it's your invitation to Him. He's coming over for a visit. And that means it's your quaint table the King of Kings wants to lounge at. He wants to hang out at your place and talk over the meal you've prepared for Him.

There have been many times where Jesus came into my prayer session, like when He walked in through my back door and nonchalantly sat on my coffee table. Often when I am driving by myself, I'll look over at the empty passenger seat and say, "Jesus, I would love it if You rode next to me, and we could talk." I then proceed to drive and converse with Jesus like I would my wife or friend. I've had similar experiences with the Father and the Holy Spirit.

God wants to be in that real and intimate kind of relationship with us. And the thing about relationships is they are two-sided. Just as much as He wants you to talk with Him, He wants you to listen to Him. He wants you to give Him your undivided attention and be quiet long enough for Him to get a word in. He is a real person and prayer should be most of all viewed as the means of intimacy with Him.

In my walk with God, I've had seasons where I talked with Him freely, and it was easy to hear Him talk with me, and I've had times where it was challenging. I have some amazing friends that seem to have no problem communicating back and forth with God all day, even arguing with Him. They hear God say things to them, and they push back like a teenager to their parent. The fact that they know He is trustworthy, and they aren't going to win any arguments, doesn't slow them down. I admire that in a way, though I don't often argue with God myself. Their relationship with Him, and the freedom that they feel to be real with Him is beautiful.

My hope and prayer for you is that your relationship with the Father, Son, and Holy Spirit would deepen and become more real. That every day you would commune with God. In the morning, He is waiting. Look at Him before your phone. Allow the Holy Spirit to replace your anxious thoughts with prayers. Praise your Heavenly Father and thank Him all through the day. As you lay your head to rest, connect with Jesus and allow Him to speak into the stillness.

Prayer

As you know, I normally include a prayer at the end of each chapter. But I think it's especially important, right now, for you to pray in your own words as you have been inspired. Don't skip this opportunity to connect with Him!

Chapter 3

Hearing God and Knowing His Will

'I know the plans that I have for you,' declares the Lord, 'plans for prosperity and not for disaster, to give you a future and a hope. Then you will call upon Me and come and pray to Me, and I will listen to you. And you will seek Me and find Me when you search for Me with all your heart.

Jeremiah 29:11-13 NASB

WHAT IS GOD'S WILL for your life? This is one of the most common questions passionate followers of

Christ have. The Bible teaches much about God's general will, like the verses we referenced in the last chapter: "Always be joyful. Never stop praying. Be thankful in all circumstances, for this is God's will for you who belong to Christ Jesus (1 Thessalonians 5:16-19 NLT)." But scripture cannot answer all your life questions, or tell you the specific plans God has for you. Thankfully the Lord is still speaking these days—to those who will listen. Knowing, hearing, and trusting His voice will help you know and walk out His purposes for your life.

Contrary to some people's beliefs, God's will is not automatically done. This is proven easily in scripture through verses about salvation. Despite many people remaining cold toward God, 2 Peter 3:9 tells us that He is not willing for anyone to perish, but that all would come to repentance. We know that Jesus died for the sins of the whole world from John 3:16, but a few verses later Jesus says some would rather stay in darkness than come into His light (John 3:19-20). In Matthew 23:37, Jesus is expressing His will to gather the children of Jerusalem, but laments at their refusal. It's clear that God's will to save the whole world, is circumvented by each individual's personal choice.

Understanding the truth about God's will is important. If you think whatever is happening in this world is because God directed it, you'll be inhibited from knowing and taking part in His will being done on earth as it is in Heaven

(Matthew 6:10). You won't overcome the world's pull towards mediocrity or depravity. You're not going to fight for healing or fight the enemy, if you assume God is sending these things. If you think He's orchestrating sickness to teach you something, then stop going to the doctor. However, it would be better if you didn't need to go to the doctor because you receive Jesus as your Great Physician, and your Heavenly Father as Jehovah Rapha.

If you want further explanation of God's will regarding pain and suffering, as well as the subject of physical healing, you can check out my first two books. The bottom line is you have to learn what God wants, and then purposefully join Him as you commune with Him and step out in faith. This is a crucial key in becoming supernatural. The more you do this, the more you will transform, and the more you will transform the world. And it's not as challenging as you might think. In fact, I'll share some simple tips anyone can do. Bear with me as this chapter will be a bit longer in order to cover what is needed.

The Sheep Know the Voice of their Shepherd

Jesus said, "He goes before them; and the sheep follow Him, for they know His voice. Yet they will by no means follow a stranger, but will flee from him, for they do not know the voice of strangers... My sheep hear My voice, and I know them, and they follow Me. And I give them eternal life, and they shall never perish; neither shall anyone snatch them out of My hand (John 10:4-5, 27-28 NKJV)." This wonderful promise from scripture shows that Jesus is our Great Shepherd, and He declares we know His voice, and can discern it from those who would lead us astray.

There are so many Biblical examples of people talking with God and hearing Him talk to them. But I've run across many people who doubt their ability to hear God. Even seasoned veterans at following His voice go through seasons where the enemy tells them they got it wrong, or that God isn't talking with them anymore. If you've ever thought, *I can't hear God.* It's important that you renew your mind to God's Word and cancel any agreement you've made with lies from the enemy. Simply repent and say, "The Bible says Jesus's sheep know His voice. I am His sheep, and He is my Shepherd. Therefore, I can hear God!"

> *"Go out and stand before me on the mountain," the Lord told him. And as Elijah stood there, the Lord passed by, and a mighty windstorm hit the mountain. It was such a terrible blast that the rocks were torn loose, but the Lord was not in the wind. After the wind there was an earthquake, but the Lord was not in the*

> *earthquake. And after the earthquake there was a fire, but the Lord was not in the fire. And after the fire there was the sound of a gentle whisper."*
> 1 Kings 19:11-12 NLT

One reason people miss the voice of God is because it's often less than booming—more like a gentle whisper. This is called God's still, small voice. It's easiest to hear as you seek the Lord in solitude, stilling your thoughts and listening intently. It's that simple. Ask the Holy Spirit what He wants to say, and then close your eyes and quiet your anxious mind. As you listen, don't forget to also "watch," with your physical eyes closed. Because He's not only going to speak things, He's also going to show you things (Habakkuk 2:1-3).

As you get alone with your Shepherd, ask Him questions. You should say things like, "God, what is your plan for my life?" Or, "What do you want me to do today?" Or, "Jesus, what's on your heart?" Ask what you will! He delights in spending time with you. Wait on Him and see what He says. When He speaks or begins to show you something, you can also ask for more information. We read of prophets asking God for help understanding even in the midst of visions and supernatural encounters. You too can respectfully ask God to explain things or show you more.

Becoming Supernatural

Confirmation Through the Bible, Godly Counsel, Peace, and Considering What Obedience Would Bring

God speaks by His Spirit, and we "hear" it in a similar way to our own soul's voice, as well as voices of evil spirits. Because it all can sound like our thoughts, we might not realize God is speaking or that the enemy is manipulating us. Therefore, it's imperative that we are really submitted to Jesus, and know God's character, especially through the Bible. After reading the whole Bible a few times, we understand God's ways and plans for humanity much better. We will not only have knowledge, but revelation of His goodness regarding His purposes in us, because we've seen His kindness, love, faithfulness, mercy, and grace towards His people in His written Word. Below we'll cover some other ways of testing the spirit (1 John 4:1).

We would do well to seek wise godly counsel as we attempt to hear and follow God (Proverbs 19:20 and Psalms 37:30-31). This may come from a leader in your church or a trustworthy friend who is ahead of you in their walk with Christ. If you feel peace, confide in them when you believe that you have heard from God on a matter, and ask their advice. Just be careful that you don't get in a situation where someone is trying to control you. In the end it should be your own decision and relationship with the Lord that leads you (1 Timothy 2:5 and 1 John 2:27). But if you have the option, wise counsel is invaluable.

For more assurance that you've truly heard God, ask Him in your heart (just between you and Him) for confirmation. Ideally it would be in a way that only He could show you, without your manipulation or "help." Begin looking for that confirmation. He wants to make His plans and voice clear to you, even more than you want to be led by Him. He may use that godly counsel from someone you trust. Or He may speak through scripture, or through someone's preaching you're listening to, through worship songs, through colleagues, or even in circumstances.

Sometimes you will need to make a quick decision when God's will isn't obvious and you don't have time to wait for an answer, confirmation, or godly counsel. Trust that you are a child of God and His Spirit is leading you (Romans 8:9, 14). Even if you make a mistake in good conscience, God will be able to course-correct you and help you in the aftermath. It's often helpful to follow His peace when making choices (Philippians 4:6-7). As well as considering the root of a nudging you feel can help you discern where it came from and what your response should be. You might be able to judge quickly when imagining what the outcome would be if you took action. Could it be based on a self-seeking motivation? Or would it please God, build up His kingdom, and help others?

If you are leaning toward something you desire, or it makes sense to your human understanding, it may just be your own thoughts and feelings. Likewise, if it is rooted in pride or selfish ambition. It isn't necessarily evil spirits, but sometimes our own soul leading us and speaking in answer to our questions. However if there's something spoken to you which would lead to another person or yourself being hurt in an ungodly way, it's definitely the enemy and should be treated as such. Evil spirits will pretend to be angels of light or God Himself. Sometimes they will come to you in less obvious ways to lead you astray from following God.

This is why it's helpful to think of where your action steps would lead. Is the prompting you feel something you wouldn't normally consider, that would end up being a blessing to others? Is it born out of self-sacrifice and honoring God's Kingdom and purposes on the earth? This could be God's subtle leading. Even if it leads to your own blessing, it could be emanating from Jesus's great love for you. He will take you down paths that will break off orphan spirits, or poverty and lack. This is both for your good and the good of His kingdom, but you might not seek these things on your own.

John W. Nichols

Maturing in Your Motives, Discernment, and Handling What You Hear

As you get more and more experience of listening to God in your prayer life, you will begin to hear and discern His voice more and more. You will be able to tell if you are hearing Him, if your soul is making something up, or if it's actually the enemy's lying tongue. You will mature in your relationship with God, which will purify your motives, and help you to do mighty exploits as you seek first His kingdom.

Maintain your relationship with Him above all else. The enemy is actively seeking for Christians to fall into the trap of listening to familiar spirits, and even unknowingly practicing witchcraft or divination. Don't treat your Heavenly Father like the world treats fortune tellers, horoscopes, Magic Eight Balls, Ouija Boards, tarot cards, or whatever else they are doing these days. Our motives should be more in line with laying down our lives at His feet, than seeking confirmation to go after worldly pleasures. And we should be careful not to use "His still, small voice" to manipulate the people in our lives.

If you don't seem to be hearing anything. Wait patiently, continue to trust and seek God daily, and give Him room to speak. Make sure there isn't anything

Becoming Supernatural

negatively affecting your spiritual sensitivity or your relationship with Him. Sometimes we're simply asking the wrong questions, it's not the right timing, or it may be a season where He is teaching us to be disciplined and continue in what we know we're supposed to be doing. A good thing to check is if you've been obedient to the last thing you heard Him say. We have a responsibility when He speaks, and we are often called to action.

You will become supernatural, as you mature in knowing what to do at the sound of His voice and as you grow in faith-filled obedience. Sometimes what He says is for your ears only, like the sharing of a close friend's heart, or so you can pray with greater clarity. He might speak into your spirit so you can prophesy over a situation or to someone who needs a genuine word from God. And often His words will be like a caring father's direction, not only in the secret place, but also in the world like Jesus modeled for us so well.

> *... your ears will hear a word behind you, saying, This is the way; walk in it, when you turn to the right hand and when you turn to the left.*
> Isaiah 30:21 AMPC

So go, and change the world as you follow the voice of your Shepherd!

Prayer

Jesus, You are my Shepherd, I am Your sheep, and You have promised that I am able to know and follow Your voice. Please unlock and activate my spiritual senses, and give me a gift of faith to believe that I can hear and see what You want to speak and show me. Holy Spirit, would You impart to me Your gift of discerning of spirits, that I would not follow any ungodly voice? Father, please reveal and remove anything blocking my spiritual senses, and any demonically inspired motivations. Please bless me with encounters from You. I will seek You, God. And I believe that You will reward my seeking with Your presence and richness in our relationship. Thank You, that I can hear Your voice and know Your will! In Jesus's name I pray, amen.

Chapter 4

God's Glorious Word

*And **the Word** became flesh, and dwelt among us; and we saw His glory, glory as of the only Son from the Father, full of grace and truth.*

John 1:14 NASB (emphasis added)

"A MAN IS ONLY as good as his word." This expression is quite true, even in reference to God. Numbers 23:19 says, "God is not a man, that He should lie, Nor a son of man, that He should repent. Has He said, and will He not do? Or has He spoken, and will He not make it good (NKJV)?" Praise God! He is trustworthy, and we can rely on His good word!

As we consider the word of God we should think of it in a few different ways. It is His spoken word, in the here and now, by His still small voice into your heart. And it's His recorded word which was written in the Bible. But it's most amazingly revealed in the Gospel of John, that Jesus is God's Word in the flesh. God spoke, and through Jesus His Word, everything came into existence (Colossians 1:15-17).

Jesus is the perfect representation of God, His living, breathing Word. Similar to Jesus, the Bible also reflects God, breaking into our realm with the gift of revelation. It is who He is in written form. That is amazing, and if it doesn't make you want to read the Bible, I don't know what will!

In the previous chapter, we talked about listening to God's still small voice and hearing His Word. If you ever feel like you can't hear Him, just read the Bible. God has spoken, but so many continue to let His Word collect dust. He spoke to people and through people. And they wrote those inspired words which became the Bible. Amazingly, we are able to continue receiving from God, no matter how many times we have read His written Word.

As a new believer, I was surprised to learn what we have today is actually a compilation of 66 books, written over the course of a few thousand years, by several Holy Spirit-led authors. Eventually these writings were put together into an agreed upon book by the early Christians.

The Old Testament is comprised of ancient Hebraic scrolls testifying of, and foretelling, God's work. It includes many kinds of writing from prophetic poetry, to wise proverbs, and divinely inspired historical records. All these point to YHWH (the holy name of God in Hebrew), the maker of the heavens and the earth, and His interactions with mankind.

Meanwhile the New Testament, written in Greek and Aramaic, is made up of various delightful letters, testimonials, encouragements, and revelations penned by men under the anointing of the Most High. These show how Yeshua Hamashiach (Hebrew for Jesus the Messiah) fulfilled the law and the prophets of the Old Testament, and His rescue mission to redeem humanity. The New Testament also reveals who we are meant to be today and expands upon the Old Testament story of what is coming in the future.

There were some other books included in the binding of the Bible until recent history, which we will likely touch on during this series. Even though they are considered extra-Biblical, they are referenced by scripture and it's clear that Jesus and His contemporaries were familiar with them. Looking at them in light of the Bible reveals some things that are hinted at but not explained in scripture, and were understood by the inspired writers of the Word of God. However, in this book, we are focusing on what is agreed to be the canonized Holy Bible, and how to apply its truth with the help of His Spirit.

Becoming Supernatural

Receiving God's Daily Bread

The amazing book of Exodus tells of God rescuing the children of Israel from Egyptian slave-masters, the provision of His loving commandments, and part of the time they spent as nomads before entering the promised land. Chapter 16 depicts the beginning of a period when God provided a mysterious bread from Heaven, called manna. The followers of Jehovah had to trust Him daily for this bread, as it would spoil if they tried to store it, except for when God said to gather and store twice the daily portion in preparation for the weekly sabbath rest (Exodus 16:1-31).

Fast forward about a thousand years and Jesus tells His disciples to pray for daily bread (Luke 11:3). He also miraculously fed over 5,000 people with five barley loaves and two small fish, and said, "Moses did not give you the bread from heaven, but My Father gives you the true bread from heaven. For the bread of God is He who comes down from heaven and gives life to the world."

Then they said to Him, "Lord, give us this bread always."

And Jesus said to them, "I am the bread of life. He who comes to Me shall never hunger, and he who believes in Me shall never thirst (John 6:32-35 NKJV)."

It can't be said enough that we need to have a habit of connecting with Jesus and reading His Word daily. We've established that both Jesus and the Bible are the Word of God, and though this precious Word will never spoil, we must receive it daily for our true nourishment.

Whether you get up a few minutes early to read, or during breaks at work, or every night before bed—your habitual practice of reading the Word will gradually transform you. In the workbook action steps from Chapter 1, I said that reading four chapters daily will facilitate finishing the whole Bible in one year. I read slowly, so it takes me about twenty minutes per day, which is a really minuscule amount of time. However much time you invest is worth the immeasurable value you will gain.

While I plead for you to get a physical Bible and use it, I must also admit there are many helpful and free apps that include a plethora of Bible translations, devotionals, and reading plans. All of these you can have with you at all times on your phone. Still, don't throw away your paperback, hardcover, or leather-bound Bible, because who knows how long those apps will be freely available or who might be able to easily change the words within them.

The main idea is that you are intaking the Word of God on a regular basis. There have been times where I followed a reading plan and times when I didn't. Often I ask the Holy Spirit to tell me what He wants me to read. He'll bring little snippets of scripture to my mind, and I'll go and look them up and read the context. I might even find myself reading the whole chapter, or that whole book of the Bible in one sitting. All because the Holy Spirit spoke.

Tips for Understanding the Word of God

As you make a habit of reading scripture, there are some practical things to consider. It's actually a good practice to read entire books of the Bible in one sitting when possible. Some of the books are probably too large to do that, but a lot of the books you can read pretty quickly. That's how many of these books were intended to be read. They didn't have verse numbers, chapters, and subheadings in the original manuscripts. They weren't meant to be read one verse at a time. The more context you are able to read in one sitting will give you a bigger picture and greater understanding than if you only read a few sentences.

Don't get me wrong, I'm not one who believes you should never read one verse at a time, out of context. Or that a pastor can't preach and reference small passages of the Bible effectively. When you read the Bible, you will find it often quotes itself out of context, with references to little phrases that are now understood in a completely different light than the original context. But in talking about having a full understanding, we need the macroscopic as well as the microscopic views.

As you read regularly, you will grow in understanding how parts of the Old Testament point to parts of the New Testament and how it all fits together. You can also begin to understand the metaphorical and prophetic insights, such as certain people and ideas from the Bible being types or representations of a deeper eternal truth. For instance, as Abraham was told to sacrifice Isaac, we can see how it foreshadowed God being willing to give His only Son as a sacrifice for us to be saved. Hebrews tells us that the temple in Jerusalem was designed after the true temple in Heaven. Even as King David was writing seemingly from his own perspective in the Psalms, his experiences at times prophetically spoke of Jesus.

You might be tempted to think that these things are hard to comprehend, but don't fall for the lie that you can't understand the Bible. It truly can be easily understood by almost everyone. In Jewish culture, children ages seven and older were expected to be taught the law from scripture and to hear the books of Moses read to them. This is the first five books of the Bible, also called the Pentateuch. With the Holy Spirit inside, you are even more equipped to receive His Word.

Too often, people have received a lie that they can't read and understand the Bible. Sometimes there's also demonic influence that causes them to feel unmotivated, sleepy, easily distracted, or even scrambling the words of scripture

Becoming Supernatural

when they try to read. This is not a hopeless situation, the person only needs to declare the truth, and command whatever is coming against them to leave in the name of Jesus. If the trouble continues, they shouldn't feel ashamed or condemned, but get help from a fellow believer who has experience walking in the authority Christ has given us.

Most importantly, value the Bible as the Word of God, and the Holy Spirit as the one who helps you understand it. More than we need man's interpretation and man's explanation of the Word—we need the Holy Spirit's revelation. A lot of new believers are told to read other people's commentary on scripture. While commentary can be helpful, even more helpful is the Holy Spirit's teaching within your spirit.

When I was a new believer, I really loved the Word of God, but I had some wrong ideas even as I was reading scripture. I didn't realize this until I continued reading the Bible over and over. Eventually, through the whole counsel of God (Acts 20:27), and rightly dividing the Word of Truth (2 Timothy 2:15), the Holy Spirit taught me. Then not only was I able to discern my own error, but I could tell when others didn't have a good understanding of the Bible. Whether a wound has caused a wrong idea about God, some theology has overemphasized certain things, or a wrong definition of a word has changed a passage's meaning, we need revelation from the Holy Spirit to straighten us out.

John W. Nichols

Being Transformed by God's Glorious Word

We need to discern the difference between the Word revealed by the Spirit of God in our spirit, versus what we've received in our soul. Remember our soul contains our natural understanding and the things we've learned in this world. Hebrews 4:12 tells us, "The word of God is living and powerful, and sharper than any two-edged sword, piercing even to *the division of soul and spirit*, and of joints and marrow, and is a discerner of the thoughts and intents of the heart (NKJV emphasis added)."

The difference between soul and spirit in many ways is a mystery to us. Most people can't tell the difference, but the Word of God is able to divide between soul and spirit. In other words, with the wielding of the sword of the Spirit, which is the Word of God (Ephesians 6:17), we are able to discern and separate the truth we have received by the Spirit, from the lesser and often confused understanding of our soul.

The Bible will refine and transform you. It tells you to renew your mind and be washed with water by God's Word (Ephesians 5:26 and Romans 12:1-2). It builds your faith as you hear it (Romans 10:17). And as you begin to act in faith because of the Word at work in you, then you will become more like Jesus, who exemplified a supernatural life.

Becoming Supernatural

The Word who became flesh, Jesus, was led by the Holy Spirit and allowed His Father to powerfully work through Him. He shows us this life-giving way, and He calls us to follow in His footsteps—becoming supernatural. As you embrace the truth of the spiritual realm revealed through scripture, and it's realized in your life, you are changing to become more in line with who God designed and destined you to be.

Your experience and personification are able to supersede the ways of this world, and expand into God's heavenly ways and kingdom. Then you will not only see the natural, but understand the spiritual behind it, and you will be able to effect both the natural and spiritual realities as a joint-heir with Christ and a child of God.

The Bible says in James 1 that the Word is like a mirror and we are not meant to stay the same as we look into it. When the Word speaks to us, and it cuts us, dividing soul and spirit, it's trying to transform. We need to submit because it's then that we begin to reflect the image of God. As Jesus was the Word of God made flesh, He intends our flesh to become the Word of God in the earth. In other words, our natural and spiritual life should be transformed to look like Jesus. The more that we pursue Him and we receive His Word, the more we will supernaturally reflect Him in the world.

Prayer

Jesus, thank You for being the perfect imprint and very image of God (Colossians 1:15 and Hebrews 1:3 AMPC). Thank You for humbly leaving Your throne, in order to be for us the Word of God made flesh. Thank You for showing us the way. I want to receive You, Word of God. Help me to read Your Bible regularly, like one who is seeking nourishment from daily bread. Holy Spirit, please help me to understand and be transformed by your glorious Word which is sharp and living. And please change me to supernaturally reflect the image of Christ as I see myself in the mirror of Your Word. Then I will be able to follow in Your footsteps, Jesus, and be a light to the world. Thank You, Lord! It's in Your name I pray, amen.

Chapter 5

Being Submerged in His Spirit

*... He will baptize you
with the Holy Spirit and with fire.*
Matthew 3:11b NLT

THIS IS THE MOST important chapter of the book, as becoming supernatural ultimately hinges on the baptism of the Holy Spirit. The Bible says when you believed the good news about Jesus, the Holy Spirit sealed you in Christ, as a guarantee that you are His and He is yours (Ephesians 1:13-14 and 2 Corinthians 1:21-22). This is absolutely beautiful and wonderful, but some have confused this sealing the Bible mentions with the baptism of the Spirit. And so they assume it is an automatic part of the salvation experience. However the submerging, overflowing, and empowerment of the Holy Spirit is something different and subsequent to our saving faith, and like we discussed our need for water baptism, we also need to receive this baptism into the Holy Spirit. The verses below clearly show the separation of saving faith in Jesus, water baptism, and the baptism of the Holy Spirit:

> *But when they believed Philip as he was preaching the good news about the kingdom of God and the name of Jesus Christ, both men and women were being baptized. Now even Simon (the sorcerer*) himself believed; and after being baptized, he continued on with Philip, and as he observed signs and great miracles taking place, he was repeatedly amazed.*
>
> *Now when the apostles in Jerusalem heard that Samaria had received the word of God, they sent them Peter and John, who came down and prayed for them that they would receive the Holy Spirit. (For He had not yet fallen upon any of them; they had simply been baptized in the name of the Lord Jesus.) Then they began laying their hands on them, and they were*

John W. Nichols

> *receiving the Holy Spirit*
> Acts 8:12-17 NASB (*added "the sorcerer" from v.9 for clarification).

Remember John the Baptist was speaking of Jesus when he said, "I indeed baptize you with water unto repentance, but He who is coming after me is mightier than I, whose sandals I am not worthy to carry. He will baptize you with the Holy Spirit and fire (Matthew 3:11 NKJV)." When referencing this in the last book, I briefly mentioned the need for this baptism by Jesus. We'll talk about the fire aspect in a later book. But if there's one chapter in this book that you apply, let it be this one about the baptism of the Holy Spirit.

My Personal Testimony

Around the time I had come to faith in Jesus, I was attending a church that believed the modern-day operation of the gifts of the Spirit were fake at best, and demonically inspired at worst. I was taught that the Biblical spiritual gifts ceased with the closing of the canon of scripture, using a bad interpretation of 1 Corinthians 13:8-10, and a wrong assumption that the testimonies of the baptism of the Holy Spirit in Acts only happened at that point in history, as a sign to the Jews that the gentiles were being saved.

Thankfully, it didn't take long before my own reading of scripture and the lives of people around me, testified that the gifts of the Spirit continue today and are a major blessing to those who are touched by the Lord through them.

Unfortunately, because of the fear that was instilled in me by that false theology, it was about ten years later that I experienced the gifts first-hand. This should have happened much sooner, especially since I had come to terms with the idea that these spiritual gifts were real. But I continued to have my apprehensions, and just in case you didn't know: the Lord works largely *with* our faith, and prefers not to force things on us. So what a person believes about this subject is very important. Just as I couldn't be born again before I believed, surrendered, and took a step of faith; I couldn't experience the baptism of the Holy Spirit and spiritual gifts until I was ready.

Oh how I wish I had given in sooner, as this immersion into the Holy Spirit, infilling, and overflowing, brings a further transformation and empowerment to live the life Christ died for us to live. When you're baptized in the Holy Spirit, you are going to become supernatural. Just as you see a big difference in Peter from before and after Acts chapter 2, I can testify that my life was radically changed again ten years after I had trusted in Jesus as my Lord and Savior, when I finally received the infilling of the Holy

Spirit.

Even though I wish I had accepted this blessing sooner, I'm thankful that I can speak to you from my own experience of before and after. Despite a profound and true love for Jesus, I've seen in myself and many others that the majority of the Christian life is dry and powerless until you have received the baptism of the Holy Spirit. It's a rare occasion to worship in spirit when you haven't been submerged in the Holy Spirit. Believers can at times still feel the movement of God, sense His presence, and be overcome with worship towards Him. They are worshiping Jesus in spirit and in truth, and they can still be used by the Father in wonderful ways. But there is so much more available in His Holy Spirit.

Just as the man who wanted to trust Jesus would heal his son declared, "I do believe, but help me overcome my unbelief (Mark 9:24 NLT)," I am so thankful that God didn't give up on me because of my mixture and double-mindedness on this issue. I was finally pushed over the edge one morning in 2011 as I was spending time with the Lord. I was joyfully resting in Him and waiting on Him to speak when I heard suddenly and clearly, "I want to give you the gift of tongues."

With a knee-jerk plea of, "No, Lord! If you want to give me any other gift..." the repulsion imparted into me through bad theology was exposed along with my fear of being strange.

The sweet nearness of His presence and friendship, shifted to a tangible feeling of grief in the room (Ephesians 4:30), as I heard Him ask, "How could you not want *anything* I have to offer you?"

I immediately repented and told my Savior, "I want everything You have for me." It was not long after this that I was baptized in the Holy Spirit and began to speak in other tongues (Acts 2:4). My life was never the same. And I didn't know that my wife I were entering a very trying year, where I wouldn't know how to pray. I'm thankful that I was able to pray according to the perfect will of God when I didn't have the words (Romans 8:26-27 and 1 Corinthians 14:2-5).

I began to have a greater zeal, boldness, and passion for the Lord where it was much more subdued before. I was able to spend more time in prayer. I started having prophetic dreams and mysteriously knowing things that ended up coming true. Eventually the Lord called my family into ministry and it was His Spirit that empowered us to minister healing, deliverance, and by His grace gifts listed in these verses:

- Romans 12:6-8
- 1 Corinthians 12:27-31
- Ephesians 4:11-16

I'm so thankful that Jesus brought me to that uncomfortable place, like when He asked the rich young ruler to sell all his possessions and give them to the poor (Matthew 19:16-22). He's not afraid of offending us in order to lead us into a deeper faith and walk with Him. I shudder to think of what would have happened to my life if I had turned away from the gift of His Spirit.

Endued with Power from on High

After Jesus was resurrected from the dead, we know that He ministered about 40 days, being witnessed by many and teaching on the kingdom of God (Acts 1:3 and 1 Corinthians 15:3-8). Before His ascension into Heaven, He breathed on His disciples and said receive the Holy Spirit (John 20:22), and He gave them the great commission of preaching the gospel all over the earth (Matthew 28:18-20, Mark 16:15-18, Luke 24:45-49, John 20:21-22). But another of Jesus's parting commands was recorded at the end of the Gospel of Luke and the beginning of Acts.

> *"Behold, I send the Promise of My Father upon you; but tarry in the city of Jerusalem until you are endued with power from on high..."*

> *"...wait for the Promise of the Father, "which,"*

> He said, "you have heard from Me; for John truly baptized with water, but you shall be **baptized with the Holy Spirit** not many days from now... you shall receive power when the Holy Spirit has come upon you; and you shall be witnesses to Me in Jerusalem, and in all Judea and Samaria, and to the end of the earth."
>
> Luke 24:49 and Acts 1:4b-5, 8 NKJV (emphasis added)

Jesus was preparing His disciples for ministry much like He modeled. We read in Luke 3:21-23 that Jesus did not begin His ministry until after His water baptism and the Holy Spirit's descent upon Him. He then immediately goes into the desert to fast, *filled* with the Holy Spirit, and returns afterwards in the *power* of the Holy Spirit (Luke 4:1-2 and 14-15).

We know that the disciples were praying and waiting in Jerusalem after Jesus's ascension for about 10 days until the day of Pentecost came, a Jewish feast which takes place 50 days after Passover (when Jesus had been crucified and was resurrected).

> *On the day of Pentecost all the believers were meeting together in one place. Suddenly, there was a sound from heaven like the roaring of a*

mighty windstorm, and it filled the house where they were sitting. Then, what looked like flames or tongues of fire appeared and settled on each of them. And everyone present was filled with the Holy Spirit and began speaking in other languages, as the Holy Spirit gave them this ability.
Acts 2:1-4 NLT

They must have been having a lot of joy, and probably a raucous good time because they were accused of being drunk! But Peter responded, "These people are not drunk, as some of you are assuming. Nine o'clock in the morning is much too early for that. No, what you see was predicted long ago by the prophet Joel: 'In the last days,' God says, 'I will pour out my Spirit upon all people. Your sons and daughters will prophesy. Your young men will see visions, and your old men will dream dreams. In those days I will pour out my Spirit even on my servants—men and women alike—and they will prophesy (v.15-18 NLT)."

Then this man who recently denied he knew Jesus three times in the hours leading up to His torture and crucifixion, Peter, continues boldly preaching about Jesus, ultimately proclaiming, "Each of you must repent of your sins and turn to God, and be baptized in the name of Jesus Christ for the forgiveness of your sins. Then you will receive the gift of the Holy Spirit. This promise is to you, to your children, and to those far away—all who have been called by the Lord our God (v.38-39 NLT)." In response to the words of this man on fire, and filled with the Holy Spirit, about 3,000 people came to faith!

The testimonies of the baptism and the power of the Holy Spirit continue throughout Acts. In the next two chapters, Peter and John heal a lame man in the name of Jesus, stand up to the Jewish leaders, and are filled *AGAIN* with the Holy Spirit along with other believers who were praying for boldness (Acts 4:29-31). Just a few verses later we read:

> *At the hands of the apostles many signs and wonders were taking place among the people; and they were all together in Solomon's portico. But none of the rest dared to associate with them; however, the people held them in high esteem. And increasingly believers in the Lord, large numbers of men and women, were being added to their number, to such an extent that they even carried the sick out into the streets and laid them on cots and pallets, so that when Peter came by at least his shadow might fall on any of them. The people from the cities in the vicinity of Jerusalem were coming together as well, bringing people who were*

> *sick or tormented with unclean spirits, and they were all being healed.*
> Acts 5:12-16 NASB

There are too many testimonies like this to share in one chapter. And it continues to happen in other believers, not just Jesus's original disciples. My point is, the Holy Spirit's baptism is what's needed to be able to accomplish these things. Just as Jesus told them to wait until they were endued with power from on high, we too need to be empowered to be His witnesses and for there to be miraculous signs accompanying the gospel. Whether those musty religious theologians believe it or not, these types of things are continuing to happen today. If you haven't seen them personally yet, I want to stoke your faith that, "This promise is to you, to your children, and to those far away—all who have been called by the Lord our God (Acts 2:39 NLT)."

What is Our Part?

One day I had a dream where Jesus asked me, "How much of the Holy Spirit do you want?" Then I saw my arms stretching out to receive the Holy Spirit, and they didn't stop expanding. I saw them stretching away from me until my arms encircled the world. And I knew Jesus was showing me I could have as much as I wanted of the Holy

Spirit who is immeasurable and inexhaustible. He said in Luke 11:9 & 13 (AMP), "Ask and keep on asking, and it will be given to you; seek and keep on seeking, and you will find; knock and keep on knocking, and the door will be opened to you... how much more will your heavenly Father give the Holy Spirit to those who ask and continue to ask Him!" So our part is first to believe and then to continue to ask the Father for this blessing, and watch what He does!

Just like we see over and over in Acts, when you get filled with the Holy Spirit, you may be overcome with a new language. It might bubble up from deep within, or it may be as subtle as a strange word on your mind. You will be able to speak in tongues, a supernatural language that is unable to be understood without the Holy Spirit's gift of interpretation, but nonetheless powerful to build you up and pray God's perfect will. We see in 1 Corinthians 14 that Paul clearly shows he could choose when he spoke in tongues and when he didn't. In other words, it wasn't when he was taken over by the Holy Spirit apart from his control. Likewise you will not lose control of your mouth, and you will have to submit your tongue, and begin to speak in faith. This is also a part of our own responsibility as we operate initially and grow in the gifts of the Spirit. It takes submitting our body, soul, and spirit in faith and discipline.

Remember that our understanding is not as necessary as we might think. The most important thing is to be submitted to God, doing His will by the power of the Holy Spirit, and with His leading. When you do this, you will be imparted with a supernatural desire and ability for evangelism, authority to overcome the enemy, and an unlocking of the spiritual gifts the Bible talks about. But you still have a part to play, of faith, obedience, and discipline. So I encourage you to continue seeking the Father for His promise of being endued with power from on high, and speak forth the mysteries of the Spirit through the Holy Spirit enabled gift of tongues. Continue in these and the other supernatural footsteps of Jesus and you will see wonderful things!

Prayer

Father, thank You for sending Your Spirit to the world. Thank You for sealing me with the Holy Spirit until the day of redemption. Thank You Jesus for showing me how to live a life empowered by the Holy Spirit and how your disciples also showed your intention for these grace gifts to continue throughout the generations until You return. I want to be one who follows You in faith, not looking to my own understanding or strength. But trusting in Your Word and waiting for You to do with me what You have done with so many others. I will continue to believe, ask, and receive for the empowering of Your Spirit. I thank You for this baptism and the subsequent fillings I will receive from You. And I will step out in faith and discipline as I recognize You are moving in and upon my life. It is all for Your kingdom and glory. In Jesus's name I pray. Amen!

Chapter 6

The Secret Place of Meeting with God

"Lord, you are my secret hiding place, protecting me from these troubles, surrounding me with songs of gladness! Your joyous shouts of rescue release my breakthrough."
Pause in his presence
I hear the Lord saying, "I will stay close to you, instructing and guiding you along the pathway for your life. I will advise you along the way and lead you forth with my eyes as your guide. So don't make it difficult; don't be stubborn when I take you where

> *you've not been before. Don't make me tug you and pull you along. Just come with me!"*
> Psalms 32:7-9 TPT

Your Father Who is in the Secret Place

I USED TO MEET with Almighty God, maker of the heavens and the earth, in my closet. That may sound strange to some, but it's actually Biblical. Jesus said, "When you pray, go into your inner room, close your door, and pray to your Father who is in secret; and your Father who sees what is done in secret will reward you (Matthew 6:6 NASB)."

The context of this verse is about when people are praying in front of an audience, and they are more concerned with impressing them than giving God true honor, genuine praise, and heartfelt worship. Our intentions shouldn't be swayed by what anyone else is thinking as we approach God. The moment we do this, whether in church or anywhere else, we have taken our focus off our Heavenly Father and our motives have become mixed.

We should only have eyes for Him, especially during times of prayer, praise, and worship. As much as possible, we shouldn't be concerned with what everyone else is thinking. It doesn't matter if they're looking at us, if they're impressed by us, or if they're judging us. Especially as we step into leadership positions, we need to take extra precautions to keep our hearts pure, remembering always that our audience is with the King.

I would still be humbly meeting with God, kneeling with my face to the ground in my closet, but we only have wardrobes where we live in Italy! That doesn't stop me from finding secret places to meet with Him. I'm not trying to impress anyone as I say these things. But I hope to inspire and lead people to also meet with God regularly—and worship Him in spirit and in truth.

Early in the morning, secreted away at midday, or in the middle of the night. In the mountains, or the woods, or the kitchen—wherever you can meet without distractions—close the door and just talk with your Creator. Just listen. Just rest in His presence. Commune with Him who knows you better than anyone else and loves you with an everlasting love. As you seek Him in the secret place, He will reward you openly.

> *"He who dwells in the secret place of the Most High Shall abide under the shadow of the Almighty. I will say of the Lord, "He is my refuge and my fortress; My God, in Him I*

> will trust..."
>
> "Because he has set his love upon Me, therefore I will deliver him; I will set him on high, because he has known My name. He shall call upon Me, and I will answer him; I will be with him in trouble; I will deliver him and honor him. With long life I will satisfy him, And show him My salvation."
> Psalm 91:1-2; 14-16 NKJV

The psalms show us not to hide ourselves from the Lord, even our sin. But as we come openly, we also invite Him to come and be real with us. In those places He heals us. As we expose and give to Him the things that are broken, hurting, and sinful, He doesn't reject us but brings freedom and restoration. He sings songs of deliverance over us. I love that. I'm not too proud to think I don't need deliverance. No, I need to repent of what is not of Him and receive His rescue, peace, and love. "As the deer longs for streams of water, so I long for you, O God. I thirst for God, the living God. When can I go and stand before him (Psalm 42:1-2 NLT)?"

Priceless Treasure in Jars of Clay

Though we are weak, as we remain connected to the vine

that is Jesus, receiving His daily bread, regularly meeting with Him, we start to look like the one we are worshiping. His Spirit is filling us like anointing oil in a jar, and we are able to pour out in ministry in ways we're incapable of on our own. We never run out of oil because we are refilled through our continual intimacy with the Lord. The Bible describes our bodies as clay jars, and His Spirit as the oil. This precious, powerful treasure of His Spirit is housed in humble and weak earthen vessels—so that He gets the glory.

> *"For God, who said, "Light shall shine out of darkness," is the One who has shone in our hearts to give the Light of the knowledge of the glory of God in the face of Christ. But we have this treasure in earthen vessels, so that the surpassing greatness of the power will be of God and not from ourselves; we are afflicted in every way, but not crushed; perplexed, but not despairing; persecuted, but not forsaken; struck down, but not destroyed; always carrying about in the body the dying of Jesus, so that the life of Jesus also may be manifested in our body. For we who live are constantly being delivered over to death for Jesus' sake, so that the life of Jesus also may be manifested*

in our mortal flesh."
2 Corinthians 4:6-11 NASB

In Matthew 25:1-13, Jesus tells a parable about ten virgins with oil lamps waiting to come to a marriage feast. Some of them, described as wise virgins, had enough oil to last through the night as they waited for the bridegroom. But some, described as foolish, ran out of oil because they didn't bring enough. When the bridegroom was delayed, the foolish virgins tried to get oil from others, but they weren't able to in time for the marriage feast. When they tried to get into the feast, the bridegroom said he didn't know them.

Even when it seems He's far away, even when you feel exhausted, the oil you have built up through relationship with Jesus will help you to carry on through the dark night season. You will continue to have oil to pour out. You will continue to be able to minister to the people around you. You will continue to stay in close fellowship with God, even though you may not understand what you're going through. You know the truth that He is with you. You know that He promised never to leave you or forsake you. And so you keep up this intimacy, this filling of oil, and your fire stays lit.

This oil represents the Spirit of God who fills us through our relationship with Jesus, and the fire represents the purification He brings. We need to meet with Him in the secret place daily, continuing to build our intimacy, even when we can't sense His presence. Our regular commitment shows how we value Him. And through it, we will always have oil in our lamp and our fire can burn through the night. The oil of His Spirit empowers a supernatural life, His light shines out of us for the world to see, and His anointing is upon us to minister to those who come to the light.

Closing with Another Example of Praying Scripture

In Chapter 2 we talked about using scripture to pray, and I shared a prayer based on Hebrews 5:11-14 AMP. As we close this chapter, we will pray another prayer about being one who worships Jesus in spirit and in truth, and invites Him to come into you, based on Psalms 24:3-10 and Revelation 3:15-22 NKJV. This is about being cleansed and coming into the presence of God, so that you can overcome the world. And ultimately, it's about having a secret place in your spirit where you and the Lord commune.

The Holy Spirit showed me the correlation between these passages after several days of fasting. Both of these parts of scripture speak of being purified by the Lord and inviting Him in. I believe the ancient gates that are called to be opened to the King of Glory in Psalms 24 are the doors of people's innermost being. Ephesians 1:3-6 reveals that He chose us in Christ before the foundation of the world; I would say that means our spirits are pretty ancient! Revelation 3 says that Jesus is knocking on the door, and if we open it—He will come into us!

Prayer

I desire to ascend into the hill of the Lord and stand in His holy secret place. Lord, please give me clean hands and a pure heart. Help me not lift up my soul to an idol or swear deceitfully. Thank You for providing a way for me to receive blessing from the Lord, and righteousness from the God of my salvation. I desire to be of the generation who seeks You, seeks Your face. I lift up my head, and the gate of my heart! The ancient part of me chosen in You before the foundation of the world (Ephesians 1:4) be lifted up, everlasting doors of my spirit! And the King of glory shall come in. Who is this King of glory? The Lord strong and mighty, The Lord mighty in battle.

I lift up my head, and the gate of my heart! Lift up, everlasting door of my spirit! And the King of glory shall come in. Who is this King of glory? The Lord of hosts, He is the King of glory. Amen.

God, please fill me with the oil of Your Spirit and stoke Your fire within me, so that when You look upon my works, I would be found aflame for you. I do not want to fool myself into thinking I'm without need. I receive your counsel and buy from You gold refined in the fire, that I may be rich; and I buy from You white garments, that I may be clothed, that the shame of my nakedness may not be revealed; and I anoint my eyes with Your eye salve, that I may see. Thank You for Your loving rebuke and chastening. Help me to be zealous and repent. Help me to hear Your knocking on the door of my innermost being. Help me to hear Your voice and open the door. Come in, King of Glory, let us meet in the secret place and commune. Help me to overcome, that I might sit with You on Your throne, just as You overcame and sat down with Our Father on His throne. Help me, Lord, to have ears to hear what the Spirit is saying. In Jesus's name, amen!

(Prayers based on Psalms 24:3-10 and Revelation 3:15-22 NKJV)

Chapter 7

Foundations of Reality from the Old Testament

In the beginning God created the heavens and the earth. The earth was without form, and void; and darkness was on the face of the deep. And the Spirit of God was hovering over the face of the waters.
Then God said, "Let there be light"; and there was light.
Genesis 1:1-3 NKJV

THE BIBLE IS A supernatural book. It took me many years of reading it to really understand the meaning, and even what happens in its pages. In this chapter I want you to learn about some of the big events of the Old Testament, which set the stage for our understanding of reality through a supernatural lens. Let's face it, I will not be able to do this justice in one chapter (even with it being as long as it is), so please forgive me in advance. I will not be able to include many, many amazing parts of the Old Testament.

But I hope to setup a foundation which will help you understand who God is, who our enemy is, and who we are. We'll really get to understand the first two of those things better in this chapter, and continue with our identity in the next chapter as I outline the New Testament. My attempt to lay it out this way is because these things are not explained in one place in the Bible, but put together from pieces of scripture.

A Simple Time-line and the Story of History

It can be a bit challenging to understand the time-line while reading the normal format of the Old Testament. This is because the sequence of events is scattered, told from multiple different perspectives, in different books, which are not placed chronologically. There are Chronological Bibles available for purchase, with all the verses of the canonized scripture formatted in the order that events took place (to the best of the publisher's ability of putting these in order). I highly recommend reading it in this way if you can, as well as the normal way of reading the books as they are placed in the Bible.

But I wanted to make a simple time-line with a limited number of important events for those who do not have a Chronological Bible or a resource like this. I will give Genesis the most attention since it encompasses a large period of time and sets things up. There are probably better resources for this, but one of the major goals of this book is to equip you in worshiping in truth, so I wanted to have something here. Please use this and the next chapter as supplements rather than replacements for reading the Bible. Although we discuss more application in the Workbook, there are still many good things I am leaving out of this chapter, including the meaning behind most of these events, and you will also get much more application as you read the actual Bible.

In a few places I will reference a couple of books which are not canonized scripture (except for in Ethiopia where some believers consider them to be scripture). I will tell why I am referencing them at that point below. These books, as well as the Apocrypha, and some other extrabiblical books have been read by believers for a long time and many consider to be beneficial. But because either the author or date of writing is not able to be confirmed, or they have aspects which conflict with doctrines or other parts of scripture, they are not considered absolute truth.

The Apocrypha are several books which are considered deuterocanonical, meaning related to the canonized scripture, and were included in the King James Bible from 1611 until 1885. Some say it's dangerous or confusing to read these and other non-canonized books, but I'd say a statement like that implies you shouldn't read anything outside of scripture, including commentaries and systematic theologies.

Just know, as you read any book like the ones I briefly mention below, you should not hold it on the same level as the Word of God. These should be considered to be more like history or stories written from a perspective that we can't claim was inspired by the Holy Spirit. I hope this helps you take it lightly, while also recognizing their historical value to believers for many hundreds of years.

Without further ado, let's jump into a simple time-line of the major events of the Old Testament.

Stories in Genesis—Creation to the Tower of Babel

- God creates the heavens and earth. In the beginning, over and over, it shows that God's creation was good. (Genesis 1)

- There is an apparent setup of angelic responsibilities, principalities on earth, powers and councils in the heavenly realms. (This is not explicitly described in scripture but many verses support it to be true. Job 1:6 & 2:1, Psalm 89:5-8, 1 Kings 22:19-23, Ezekial 28:13-14, Psalm 89:5-8, Daniel 7:9-10, Nehemiah 9:6, Revelation 4:6-11)

- God creates man and woman in His image. Responsibility is given including dominion over the earth, and they are told not to eat from the tree of the knowledge of good and evil. (Genesis 1-2, Psalm 8:3-6)

- At some point, created angelic beings like Lucifer choose to leave God's ways. Other fallen angelic hosts also disobey God and no longer do what He created them to do. (This is not described in an obvious way before Genesis 3, but is found in excerpts throughout scripture. Daniel 10:12-13, Ezekial 28:13-19, Ephesians 3:10-11, Ephesians 6:11-12, Colossians 1:16, Jude 1:6, Revelation 12:1-17, Revelation 17:1-18)

- Mankind suffers temptation to eat the forbidden fruit by a serpent in the garden. Humanity falls into sinful nature which leads to death, God comes to commune with Adam and Eve in the garden but they try to hide from Him. The serpent and the man and woman are told the consequences of their actions, and are exiled from the Garden of Eden. (Genesis 3. This serpent was originally upright and spoke, implying it was not what we think of as a snake. Revelation 12:9 calls him Satan and refers to him as a dragon.)

- Some of the children of Adam and Eve follow God and some choose the ways of sin. (Genesis 4)

- God protects a lineage of humanity until the prophecy of Genesis 3:15 can by fulfilled by Jesus. (Seen in various genealogies, culminating in Luke 3:21-38. There are also many who believe the seed of Satan is a literal lineage of corrupted humanity.)

- Because of sin the vast majority of mankind and the world is corrupted in an irredeemable way. The Nephilim (giants) are created through a type of fallen heavenly being having sexual relations with human women. Because of the abundant corruption and depravity, God decides to start over with a small group of people (the family of Noah) and animals who have remained pure. (Genesis 6. Some gloss over this aspect that is only mentioned briefly in Genesis 6, but understanding this helps a lot more of the Old Testament make sense. Some people try to explain this verse and minimize the aspect of giants, saying the sons of God were the lineage of Adam who followed God, but this word is always used in scripture to mean a directly created being like an angel, rather than a naturally begotten being like a human child. Some try to minimize the Bible's supernatural elements by claiming that the words "gods," or "mighty ones," were merely humans raised up to a governmental role, but the original language is clearly speaking of something else. In the case of Genesis 6, I believe these were literal giants that were utterly evil. Some believe that in the Garden of Eden there was also something sexual in nature similar to what's described in Genesis 6, but between the serpent and Eve, resulting in Cain being the first of the seed of Satan. The extra-biblical book of 1 Enoch quoted in Jude 1:14-15, gives more context to Genesis 6, discussing the giants, and calling the fallen angelic beings, "Watchers," who took human wives and taught mankind various patterns of sin. We will see that the name of the leader of the Watchers is mentioned later in scripture in a way that strengthens this as a quite possible part of history. According to Jude and Enoch these Watchers have been punished and are in chains now. The book of 1 Enoch is not canonized except in Ethiopia, but it was widely read during the time of Jesus and sects of Judaism before His birth.)

- A man named Noah, whose generations were pure, found favor in God's sight, is given instructions to build an ark and bring into it a certain number and type of animals, afterwards the waters come from the "great deep" and the sky to flood and destroy the earth including the rest of the living beings. (Genesis 6:9-9:17. Based on Genesis 2:5-6 and Genesis 7:4, 10-12 there was no rain on the earth before the flood. It seems that the animals needed to be ones that had not been corrupted, possibly suggesting there was a type of ungodly tampering going on with creation. Whether that is something like the hybrids we see in mythology, similar to what was happening with the Nephilim, or as simple as the hybridization that is public knowledge today, the text doesn't say. On another note, the extra-biblical book of 1 Enoch explains that demons are disembodied spirits of giants after their death in the flood, which makes more sense than other explanations I have heard. Many cultures all over the world have historical stories of a flood and mythos of giants, hybrid creatures like mermaids, minotaur, fawns, snake/human mixtures, very small human-like creatures, angels, and demons, etc.)

- After the rain stops, the water subsides, and ground dries under the ark. Noah worships God with a sacrifice. And God promises never to flood the earth again, giving the sign of the rainbow. Some of Noah's family continues to worship God, but some choose the way of sin. We see here people groups and cities which are later known for their depravity, witchcraft, worship of false gods, and the resurgence of giants. This comes through Nimrod who is in the line of Ham, "father of Canaan (who quickly exhibits sin after the flood)." (Genesis 9:18-10:32, Genesis 10:8-20. Nimrod and Gilgamesh of Sumeria are thought to be the same person under different names. The ancient secular Epic of Gilgamesh also tells the story of the flood and shows he wanted to live forever. As the Bible describes Nimrod as a "mighty one," Gilgamesh was said to be a demi-god because his mother was part "divine." Whether this is the case or not, the resurgence of giants make it apparent that the issue of genetic corruption somehow continued after the flood. Many other cultures have mythos of demi-gods, similar to the story of Nephilim/Giants being created through the sexual relations of humans with a type of fallen angelic being, which they would call a god.)

- People are of one language and begin to build the Tower of Babel, but God scatters them and confuses their language. (Genesis 11:1-9. It is believed Nimrod was a major part of the tower being built based on its location and correlation to Genesis 10:10. The extra-biblical book of Jasher mentioned in Joshua 10:12-13 and 2 Samuel 1:18-27, says Nimrod took part in building the Tower of Babel which was a sin, built against the Lord, intended to ascend into Heaven and make war with God. Jasher is not considered canon except in Ethiopia.)

- Also note, the book of Job is actually the oldest written book in the Bible. Scholars believe it took place between the flood and Abraham. Moses (who we will talk about later) wrote the first five books of the Bible including Genesis, which must have included stories passed down, as well as probably given in parts directly by God. It's not known who wrote the book of Job.

Stories in Genesis—Abraham to the Tribes of Israel

- God visits Abram, a descendant of Noah through Shem, telling him to leave his family and land, and entering into a covenant with him. He promises to make his descendants outnumber the stars. But Abram's wife, Sarai, could not physically have children. As God unfolds His promise to Abram, his name will be changed to Abraham, and he will be called the Father of Many Nations. (Genesis 11:29-30, Genesis 12-15)

- God also tells Abram prophetically, that his descendants will be in slavery, but will be brought out and will inhabit the land of Canaan. This is one of the lands populated by the descendants of Ham (and Nimrod after him) who worshiped other gods and the land became overrun by giants. (Genesis 15:13-21. The fulfillment of this prophecy is written throughout Exodus, Joshua, and some records in other Biblical books.)

- Because it seems God's promise has been delayed and Sarai still can't have children, they plan to have a child through Abram having sexual relations with their Egyptian servant Hagar, and Ishmael is born. Sarai then becomes jealous, and Hagar and Ishmael leave for a time, and the Angel of the Lord helps them and prophesies over Ishmael. Mercifully, God gives Abram and Sarai new names (Abraham and Sarah), continues to prophesy over them and Ishmael, and promises they will have a son who will be called Isaac. The act of circumcision is introduced as a sign of covenant with God. (Genesis 16-17. The Islam/Muslim religion is descended through Ishmael and they believe he is the fulfillment of God's promise to Abram. Historically, the Ishmaelites worshiped many gods until Mohammad united them under the worship of Allah. The Jewish people come through the lineage of Isaac. Meanwhile, Christians include people from all nations, and the Bible says we are grafted in as children of Abraham through Jesus's redemptive work. This is why Abraham is called the Father of Many Nations.)

- Because of great evil at Sodom and Gomorrah, the Lord decides to destroy the cities, but He and two angels talk with Abraham first. He tries to convince them not to destroy the cities on account of his relative Lot who lives there, but to spare them if there are ten righteous found. The angels go to Sodom and the men of the city try to rape them. The cities end up destroyed but Lot's family is spared. (Genesis 18-19. The extreme and perverse actions of the men of Sodom trying to have sexual relations with angelic beings likely has to do with the evil ways going back to Genesis 6. There are people in this day and age who practice sodomy as a form of Lucifer worship and witchcraft. When this practice is combined with other secret satanic rituals it is widely claimed to give demonic powers including seeing into the spiritual realm. I will explain these things more in later books. If the practitioners of this evil do not come to the true light who is Jesus Christ, not Lucifer, their practices will kill them, the ones they love, and they will continue to pay for their sin in the afterlife. They are deeply and sadly deceived about God and who Jesus really is, but He loves them and has provided for them to be saved, delivered, and healed. Many people have come out of this, testifying it is truly happening, but that Jesus has shown He is more powerful than the enemy.)

- As Abraham is 100 and Sarah around 90 years old, they have their first child miraculously, and name him Isaac. God tests Abraham to see if he trusts Him enough to give up his son. This test also probably has to do with the fact that child sacrifice was normal in the cultures surrounding Abraham, but God abhorred the evil act. The Bible says that Abraham's faith was attributed to him as righteousness, and he was called a friend of God. (Genesis 21-22, Deuteronomy 12:29-31, Psalm 106:34-48, James 2:23, Isaiah 41:8).

- Abraham and Sarah pass away. Isaac marries Rebekah and has two boys named Jacob and Esau. Jacob deceitfully takes Esau's birthright and first-born blessing. Jacob is told not to marry into the family of Canaan, but Esau intentionally does and marries Ishmael's daughter who lives among the Canaanites. (Genesis 23-28:9)

- Jacob heads out to his ancestors' land to find his wife, and on the way has a dream of angels ascending and descending a ladder going to Heaven. God speaks to him, prophesying about the continuation of His promise to Abraham, and Jacob vows to worship Him. (Genesis 28:10-22)

- Jacob finds the woman he wants to marry but ends up being tricked by her father, Laban, who wants his other daughter to be married first. Through a long period of time Jacob works to marry Laban's daughters, Leah and Rachel, and becoming very rich in the process. Because of jealousy and issues having children, the sisters also get Jacob to have sexual relations with their maidservants, resulting in Jacob having many sons. On the way back to Canaan, Jacob encounters God in the form of an angel and wrestles with Him until He will bless him. God dislocates Jacob's hip causing him to limp the rest of his life, but also changes his name to Israel. His children are going to become the twelve tribes of Israel which end up fulfilling God's covenant with Abraham. They are Reuben, Simeon, Levi, Judah, Issachar, Zebulun, Joseph, Benjamin, Dan, Naphtali, Gad, and Asher. (Genesis 29-36)

- One of Jacob's sons, Joseph, has some dreams that seem like his family will bow down to him. This angers his brothers and they sell him as a slave to the Ishmaelites (descendants of Ishmael), and convince their father that he is dead. Joseph ends up in Egypt, and after many hardships, interprets a dream by the Pharaoh which causes great prosperity in the land. The dream's interpretation leads to Pharaoh appointing Joseph as governor, and Egypt saving grain during several years of abundance, because a great famine later hits the lands for several years. (Genesis 37-41)

- God uses Joseph's position, favor, and blessing in Egypt to provide for Israel and his family during the famine. They come to Egypt for food and are reunited with Joseph (and his dream of being bowed down to is fulfilled). Israel's family moves to a part of Egypt called Goshen. Israel lives out the rest of his life there and before his death prophesies over his son's family lines, who are the tribes of Israel. (Genesis 42-50)

Other Stories in the Old Testament—Exodus to the Promised Land

- Many years pass after the last chapter of Genesis, and the Israelites have multiplied. The Hebrews (another name for the Israelites basically meaning descendants of Abraham, and the name of their ancient language) come under oppression by a Pharaoh that does not have the same appreciation for them as the Pharaoh who put Joseph in a position of power. In order to keep their numbers down he orders that all male babies are killed.

- God protects and raises up Moses, a Hebrew boy. Later He speaks to him through a burning bush sending him and his brother Aaron to deliver the Israelites from slavery. But Pharaoh refuses to let the Israelites go, and God brings plagues on Egypt. The final plague sets up the Jewish feast of Passover, and symbolically represents Jesus as the Passover lamb and blood covering.

- The Israelites are able to leave Egypt, but then Pharaoh decides to chase them with his army. This is when the sea is parted and the Israelites walk across on dry ground, and Pharaoh's chasing army is swallowed up in the sea.

- Moses and the Israelites wander the desert being led by God in a pillar of fire by night and cloud by day. Unfortunately the people continue to forget what God has done for them and complain about being in the desert. Still God provides food and water miraculously for the Israelites in the wilderness and their clothes and sandals never wear out.

- Moses remains in fellowship with God. He meets with Him on Mount Sanai, but the people fear Him. God gives Moses the Ten Commandments, other aspects of the law, and plans for a tabernacle which is a movable structure for worshiping and meeting with God. The tribe of Levi (Levites) is setup as priests, with Aaron being the High Priest, and other roles are given for duties in the tabernacle. This tribe is not included in receiving a portion of the promised land, but their portion is the Lord.

- While Moses is meeting with God, Aaron makes a golden calf image for the people to worship (which may be a type of image of the false god, Baal). This angers the Lord because they have turned away from Him to worship other gods. He wants to destroy the people and start over with Moses, but Moses convinces Him to give them more chances. When Moses comes down from the mountain he becomes so angry with the people's sinful celebration and worship of other gods, that he throws down and breaks the Ten Commandments that were inscribed by the finger of God on stone tablets. He tells those who will worship the true God to kill the others who will not, and the Levites kill 3,000 people. Moses then returns to God and pleads for their forgiveness.

- Moses continued to meet with God and desires to see His glory. On the mountain God gives Moses more instructions of the law including the Sabbath, plans to build the Ark of the Covenant, and He makes the stone tablets of the Ten Commandments again.

- When Moses comes down from the mountain, his face is shining from being in the presence of God.

- God continues to give the Israelites instructions including offerings for worship and cleansing from sin, the tabernacle is built, and the Levites begin their priestly duties. The presence of God is holy and so the priests have to follow the instructions just as God has given them. Two men do not follow the instructions and are burnt up by the fire of God's holy presence. He gives special instructions for the Day of Atonement and how the high priest will be able to enter the most holy place to offer the sacrifice and cleanse the people's guilt. (An interesting note is the scapegoat mentioned in this part of Leviticus 16 is supposed to take the sin to the wilderness of Azazel, which was the name of the leader of the fallen Watcher angels in the book of 1 Enoch, which also says to ascribe all sin to Azazel. This is not another name for Satan, but a different fallen angelic being.)

- The Old Testament sacrifice of animals would cleanse the sins of the people for a time, but was ultimately unable to keep them pure. No one was able to keep the law and stay righteous. But Jesus, who was called the lamb of God who takes away the sins of the world, was perfectly righteous. And He was not only pure, but He was also close to the heart of the Father and obedient. This led to the literal laying down of His life as a sacrifice to atone for all sins. Now we attain righteousness, not by our sacrifice, but by faith in the finished work of Jesus Christ.

- God continues to give the law and the appointed feasts to remember and celebrate what He has done for the Israelites. These include the Sabbath, the Passover, the Feast of Unleavened Bread, the Feast of Weeks (also called Shavuot and Pentecost), the Feast of Trumpets (Rosh HaShanah), the Day of Atonement (Yom Kippur), and the Feast of Tabernacles (Sukkot). Later, the Jewish people added the Festival of Light (Chanukah) and Purim.

- Before taking the people across the Jordan river into Canaan (the Promised land which God had prophesied to Abraham that they would possess), they sent some spies to go into the land. They saw the land was plentiful but there were many giants there. Ten out of twelve of the spies brought back a bad report, saying their people would die if they went into the land. Two of the spies, Joshua and Caleb, had faith and said that God would give them victory and provide for them.

- Because of the overall lack of faith God says the Israelites must continue in the desert for 40 years until the faithless generation had passed away. They fight some battles in the desert, Moses passes away, and Joshua becomes the leader of the Israelite people before they go back to the promised land.

- Led by Joshua the Israelites enter the promised land and go to their first city to take in battle. It is a city called Jericho and it has a massive wall encircling it. God gives them instructions to walk around the city and praise Him. After seven days the wall falls down and they capture the city.

- A common instruction from God is not to mix with those who worship other gods. Sometimes God told the Israelites to kill everyone in a city including children. Sometimes He would tell them not to take anything from a city or even offer it to Him in the tabernacle/temple. When I was first reading the Bible, I didn't understand some of this, because the explanations of it are dispersed throughout snippets of scripture, or talked about in extra-biblical books. I didn't know how depraved the nations were, their practices of child sacrifice, and the depths of their sexual perversion. I also didn't understand the corruption that led to the Nephilim/Giants or the spiritual elements behind Genesis 6-11. I believe in some of these cases these "people" were not redeemable. Not only because Jesus's provision of salvation had not taken place yet, but because of a deep rooted corruption in their DNA. They might have looked human, however the presence of giants reveals this is not just deception and worship of dead idols, but something that was changing these people's very humanity. This would explain God's command to even kill the children in some instances.

- In the case of Jericho, one of the Israelites named Achan took some of the things that were supposed to be destroyed or devoted to the Lord. This sin caused the Israelites to lose their next battle at the city of Ai. After the sin was discovered and dealt with, they were able to defeat the city with the Lord's help.

- The Israelites continue taking cities and dividing the land of Canaan among their tribes.

Other Stories in the Old Testament—Kings to Exiles

- After Joshua's passing, for some time the Israelites were led by various judges, who were like great leaders and/or warriors. Then they told God that they wanted to have a human king like the other nations. Despite that God did not want this for them and warned them of the abuses that would come through human kings, He relented and setup the first king named Saul.

- The High Priest Samuel anointed Saul as king and the Spirit of God came upon him and he prophesied. He was tall, handsome, and seemed like he was going to be a good king. But he showed that he didn't have a relationship with God, calling Him Samuel's God. He made some bad choices, ultimately showing his pride, and disrespect for Samuel and God.

- Although Saul was not removed as king, God chose the next king and had Samuel anoint him. This was a seemingly obscure shepherd boy, named David. He trusted in God and ended up becoming famous in battle by killing a Philistine giant named Goliath.

- David was put in a high position in Saul's court, married Saul's daughter, became best-friends with Saul's son Jonathan, and was known as a mighty warrior because of his victory in many battles. He remains humble though, always giving God the glory, and recognizing Him as the reason for his success.

- Saul ended up becoming jealous of David and trying to kill him on many occasions. David tries to stay submitted and honoring to King Saul, but eventually must go into hiding with a group of warriors. He has opportunities to kill Saul but showing respect for God's anointed king, he restrains himself.

- Eventually Saul dies and David is made king. Because of his heart of worship, God calls him a man after God's own heart. King David wrote many of the Psalms that are in the Bible, including prophesies of Jesus. He is of the tribe of Judah, and God fulfilled prophesies by having Jesus be born in David's lineage. The modern name, Jew and Jewish people, comes from the name of the tribe of Judah.

- David continued to be a warrior his whole life. He had a group of men who fought along-side him who were giant killers. God helped him continue to fight against the remaining idol-worshippers in the promised land. He took Jerusalem from the Jebusites, and established his kingdom there. It was dubbed the City of David. The modern day Israelite flag features a "Star of David" in the center.

- David fell into sin when he lusted after a woman named Bathsheba who was married to one of his trusted warriors named Uriah. David had sexual relations with her and she became pregnant. When he couldn't cover up what he'd done, he had her husband killed, and then married Bathsheba. God sent the prophet Nathan to call out David's sin and he then repented, showing humility and a desire to stay in relationship with God.

- David and Bathsheba have a son named Solomon who becomes the next king. Whereas David was a man of war, Solomon lived a peaceful life. When God asked him what he wanted, he said wisdom to make good choices and be able to be a good ruler over Israel. Because he didn't ask for long life, or riches, or to win in battle, God gave him his request as well as riches and that no one would equal him in honor.

- Israel lived in peace during Solomon's reign as king and they were very wealthy. He built the Lord a temple made of stone in Jerusalem. Solomon's wisdom was renown and he wrote the Biblical books of Proverbs, Song of Solomon, and Ecclesiastes.

- Unfortunately Solomon took many wives and was led astray into the worship of other gods. Freemasonry and Kabbalah (so-called Jewish Mysticism) supposedly date back to his time. These false religions are shrouded in deception, include many occult practices, and ultimately lead to the worship of Lucifer. We'll talk more about them in a later book.

- Solomon's son Rehoboam was established as the next king, but did not lead with wisdom. The kingdom of Israel becomes divided, with ten tribes in the North continuing to be called Israel under a king named Jeroboam. And the Southern tribes of Judah and Benjamin, being united under the name of Judah and led from Jerusalem by Rehoboam (Solomon's son). Jeroboam made other temples in Bethel and Dan and setup golden calves to be worshiped there (again, these were likely connected to the worship of Baal).

- Israel and Judah continue to be divided. Israel has unrighteous kings over and over, who allow and propagate the worship of other gods. The Bible shows that the One True God is jealous after the nation, as they were intended to be one nation who worshipped Him rather than the creation and the fallen angelic beings.

- Despite the unrighteous kings, God continues to raise up prophets who speak and write what He is saying. They work miracles, have visions, display signs of God, declare the thoughts and heart of God, call for repentance, and prophesy about the future (including many events that have already been fulfilled). Some of these are Elijah, Elisha, Isaiah, Jeremiah, and Ezekial; but there are many more. They each have amazing stories, but for the sake of brevity I will not be able to include them here.

- Only a few kings of Judah put a stop to the worship of other gods on the high places. These are Josiah, Hezekiah, and possibly Jehoshaphat. They not only worshipped God themselves, but they also fought against the worship of false gods by their people. When each of them were in leadership, the nation experienced blessings.

- Eventually because of the kings' and peoples' continual rejection of God, the kingdom of Assyria destroys and takes captive the Northern kingdom of Israel. Later God also allowed the Babylonian kingdom to take Judah into captivity. They end up destroying the prominent buildings in Jerusalem including the temple there. The Bible describes these events as God's way to get the people to repent and come back to Him, and He promises to restore them and their land.

- While the people of Judah are exiled in Babylon, a prophet named Daniel is one who remains true to God and continues to worship Him. They continue in exile until a prophecy is fulfilled about King Cyrus of the Persians defeating the Babylonians.

- Some Persian leaders end up allowing Ezra and Nehemiah to take Jewish people to return to Jerusalem and rebuild. The 2nd temple is built, scrolls of the law are found and proclaimed, and the walls and cities are rebuilt and resettled for a time.

- There are many prophesies about God's plans for the Israelite/Jewish people. Eventually, many of those prophesies are fulfilled in the person of Jesus.

We will break here with the Old Testament and continue with an outline of the New Testament in the next chapter. Just so you are aware, the canonized scripture has about a 400 year gap between the Old Testament and the

New Testament. There are other non-canonized books, like Macabees, which record events between this point in the Old Testament and when Jesus was born. As stated before, they are not to be regarded as divinely-inspired scripture, and are not necessary to our faith as Christians, but they may still be helpful to read.

In Summary

We see in all of this, that God created everything good. And despite the fall, He continues to love and fight for His creation. He jealously desires His people's worship and is utterly grieved and angered by any hint of worship of false gods. Even though the enemy's work is abundant, God has had a plan to overcome, and save mankind. We'll see that more in the next chapter.

You may be tempted to think that the cosmic struggles of the Old Testament stopped somewhere in history, but we must be vigilant. Although these things are not as apparent to the Western mindset, they continue to operate in sly ways. Jesus said to His disciples in Matthew 10:16 (AMPC), "Behold, I am sending you out like sheep in the midst of wolves; be wary and wise as serpents, and be innocent (harmless, guileless, and without falsity) as doves." We continue to need this advice, because our struggle with supernatural forces is just as real today as it ever was.

Thankfully, He has overcome and we are more than conquerors in Christ!

Prayer

Father God, thank You for creating everything good, both what is seen and unseen. I believe in Your goodness, despite the evil that perverted Your creation in the hidden spiritual realms, and the natural world. Thank You for Your patience with mankind, which has been exhibited over and over as Your plans are revealed and come to pass. Please help me to have discernment to see how the enemy has worked and is continuing to work. Even when things are not explicitly stated in scripture, help me to know what is true by Your Holy Spirit. I will not be overwhelmed by the enemy, but look forward to Your Spirit working in me, around me, and through me, as You continue bringing all things under the rule of Christ.

Chapter 8

Supernatural Scripture and Our Destiny

As you therefore have received Christ Jesus the Lord, so walk in Him, rooted and built up in Him and established in the faith, as you have been taught, abounding in it with thanksgiving. Beware lest anyone cheat you through philosophy and empty deceit, according to the tradition of men, according to the basic principles of the world, and not according to Christ. For in Him dwells all the fullness of the Godhead bodily; and

Becoming Supernatural

> *you are complete in Him, who is the head of all principality and power. In Him you were also circumcised with the circumcision made without hands, by putting off the body of the sins of the flesh, by the circumcision of Christ, buried with Him in baptism, in which you also were raised with Him through faith in the working of God, who raised Him from the dead. And you, being dead in your trespasses and the uncircumcision of your flesh, He has made alive together with Him, having forgiven you all trespasses, having wiped out the handwriting of requirements that was against us, which was contrary to us. And He has taken it out of the way, having nailed it to the cross. Having disarmed principalities and powers, He made a public spectacle of them, triumphing over them in it.*
> Colossians 2:6-15 NKJV

WE'RE CONTINUING FROM THE previous chapter, tying up our look at this supernatural book with a nice pretty bow that holds it all together. In the verses above we see one of the main resolutions of the story of scripture. It is that God has rescued mankind through Christ, tearing humanity away from the death-grips of fallen principalities and powers in the heavenly realms, and resurrected us who believe, complete in Christ, who is the fullness of God in bodily form.

The New Testament Timeline—The Story of Destiny

In the last quarter of the Bible, we see everything coming into focus on one individual which the previous three quarters of scripture have been crying out for. The Old Testament showed us a desperate need for a Savior, and now He is being revealed, but not in the way people thought. Where another warrior king was expected, we find a humble carpenter, more interested in the spiritually destitute than the Roman occupation of Israel. The first four books of the New Testament tell His story, that is really the story of our own destiny.

We see next the Book of Acts testifying of His disciples stepping into that destiny, which continued His transformation of the world. The New Testament goes on to explain what we've seen and showing us how to live it out through many letters written to groups of people and individuals. Finally, the greatest Revelation any prophet has ever seen is unfolded, revealing Our Savior in His radiant glory and His stunning plan coming to its marvelous resolution.

We'll now look at the overarching historical markers of the New Testament, while keeping in mind the practicality of it all. This deepening of our understanding of who God is, who our enemy is, and who we are, should inspire us to actually live a life similar to what we read.

The Gospels

The word gospel means good news, and the Gospels opening the New Testament tell the good news revealed in the life of Jesus from four different perspectives. I'll go into the greatest detail in the outline on these books. Three of these: Matthew, Mark, and Luke, are called synoptic gospels because they have most of the same events.

The more you read these gospels, the more you will recognize certain elements being emphasized. Matthew seems to be written with the goal of leading Jewish people to see that Jesus is the Messiah spoken of in the Old Testament. Mark is a concise edition, showing off the power of God displayed in Jesus. Luke is written from meticulously gathered information, possibly as a testimony for court. The Gospel of John is written with great revelation, from the perspective of a beloved disciple.

Jesus's early years are told in Luke 1-2 and Matthew 1-2:

- Mary, who is a virgin, but is betrothed to a man named Joseph, is visited by an angel who tells her she will become pregnant miraculously with Jesus. Meanwhile Zechariah and Elizabeth, who are supposed to be barren, become pregnant with John the Baptist. (It's interesting that God sends His hero to the earth through a woman, like the "mighty ones" of Genesis, but the assurance that she is a virgin shows it is not through a defiled sexual act. We can see how Jesus is a fulfillment of the Genesis 3:15 seed of a woman, who will crush the head of the seed of the serpent.)

- Mary and Joseph are from Nazareth, but because of a census they must travel to Bethlehem where Jesus is born, fulfilling prophecy. Angels visit shepherds declaring His birth.

- And a group of wise men who are following a star to find Jesus and give Him prophetic gifts, pass King Herod on the way and tell him of the King of the Jews. Herod is threatened by this king and seeks to kill all the boys under a certain age, but an angel warns Joseph in a dream to flee to Egypt to protect Jesus. The family returns to Nazareth when it is safe.

- At twelve years of age Jesus's family travels to Jerusalem for Passover. As they went home, Jesus remained in the temple asking questions of the teachers who were amazed by Him. When found by His family, He said He had to be in His Father's house and about His Father's business. Even at a young age, Jesus was doing what Our Father in Heaven wanted Him to do.

- Luke 2:52 says He grew in wisdom and in stature, showing He was not only God in a human body, but that He subjected Himself to the human experience, needing to learn and grow. I believe this and John 14:9-11 also shows that as He overcame temptation and performed miracles, He was doing it as a man, who was filled with the Holy Spirit, submitted and in close relationship to the Father.

Next Jesus begins His recorded ministry. I say recorded, because the Gospel of John tells us that if all His works were written the world couldn't contain the books (John 21:25).

- Around the age of 30 Jesus is baptized in water by John the Baptist. God speaks from the sky saying that He is His Son, and the Holy Spirit descends on Him in the form of a dove.

- Jesus then goes into the desert to fast for 40 days and is tempted by the devil. He overcomes him with the Word and returns in the power of the Holy Spirit.

- Jesus's ministry was primarily in the region of Galilee North of Jerusalem. He did many amazing things, but for the sake of brevity we will only list some of them here:
    - He called His disciples and knew things about them and others that no one could know naturally
    - He cared about people's suffering, healing multitudes and cast out demons with authority
    - He preached both in temples and outside
    - He stood up to religious leaders who were not leading people into a real relationship with God (Interestingly, He says they are of their father the devil, and John the Baptist calls them a brood of vipers. Because of this and their vehement desire to kill Jesus, some believe these religious leaders were literally a part of the seed of the serpent mentioned in Genesis 3.)
    - Besides the amazing healing and deliverance miracles, He performed many other miracles such as raising the dead back to life, turning water into wine, disappearing in the midst of angry mobs, calming storms, walking on water, having His disciples catch enormous amounts of fish, having His disciples pay taxes with a coin from a fish's mouth,

cursing a non-fruit bearing fig tree and it drying up, multiplying food, knowing peoples thoughts, speaking with great wisdom, walking through walls, and of course His own resurrection and ascension.

- His disciple Peter declared his belief that Jesus was the Messiah, and Jesus said it was God who revealed that to Peter

- He was transfigured on a mountain, where three of His disciples saw Him glorified and then heard the voice of God declare Him as His Son

Jesus then prepares to go into the City of David, where many thought He would take His rightful throne. The enemy never expected His victory would come through the cross instead.

- In the days leading up to Jesus entering Jerusalem, a woman named Mary worships at His feet and anoints Him with costly oil. One of His disciples, Judas, is upset and said it could have been used for the poor, but Jesus said they only had Him for a short time and it was anointing Him for burial. This passage also reveals that Judas would betray Jesus and he was a thief. This is the real reason why he didn't want the oil used on Jesus. A similar event to this happens again later in Jerusalem.

- Jesus rides into Jerusalem on a donkey colt (another fulfillment of prophecy), and at His entry He is honored as a Savior King by the people, throwing clothes on the path and cut palm branches, and shouting, "Hosanna in the highest."

- He went to the Temple and instead of making a sacrifice, He surprisingly made a whip and drove out money-changers and people who were selling offerings there. He overturned their tables, declaring they had made His Father's house a den of thieves instead of a house of prayer. Jesus spent other times in the temple as well while He was in Jerusalem. He prophesied when they destroy this temple, He will raise it up in three days. He was really speaking of His own body, but they took it to mean the Lord's Temple (which the Romans did destroy not long after in 70 A.D., and it has not yet been rebuilt. Based on other prophecies about the last days, it seems a third temple will be rebuilt in Jerusalem and the Antichrist will desecrate it and demand to be worshiped.).

- On the night of Passover and what will be called the "Last Supper," Jesus washes His disciples' feet, teaches them the greatest in the kingdom is the servant of all, and that they should love one another. He also institutes communion during the Passover meal, when He said the bread was His body broken for them and the wine was His blood shed for them.

- Jesus also shows that He knows Peter will deny Him three times before morning, and that Judas is going to betray Him. Satan enters Judas before he leaves to find the religious leaders to help them find and kill Jesus for 30 pieces of silver.

- That evening Jesus taught His disciples in a garden, praying over them and future believers, and speaking about the Holy Spirit coming after Him.

- He later prays in the garden and asked some of His disciples to pray with Him. While they fell asleep He prayed for the cup of suffering to pass by Him, but submitted to His Father's will.

- Judas leads some men from the religious leaders to Jesus and identifies Him with a kiss on the cheek. When they asked if He was Jesus, and He replied, "I am," (the name God called Himself to Moses). People were physically pushed over by what He said.

- He allowed Himself to be taken and tried by the religious leaders. They asked if He was the Messiah, to which He replied, "You have said so," and they accused Him of blasphemy. He was then taken to the Roman governor, Pontius Pilate, who ended up saying He was innocent, but gave Him over to the Jewish people who said His blood would be on their hands and their children's.

- Jesus was dressed in a purple robe, a crown of thorns was pushed onto His head, and He was beaten, spat on, and mocked. He received so many lashes that His back would have been completely shredded, fulfilling the prophecy that by His stripes we were healed. As He was then crucified next to two criminals, He said that the people should be forgiven as they didn't know what they were doing. One of the criminals next to Him mocked Him, but the other believed in Him. He told the believer that He would see him that day in paradise.

- As Jesus gave up His Spirit, the sky was darkened, the veil in the temple (closing off the Holy of Holies) was torn from top to bottom, and some dead people were resurrected out of their graves.

- Jesus's body was taken off the cross and He was laid in the tomb of a rich man who had donated it. The Jewish religious leaders requested Pontius Pilate to close and seal the tomb. A large stone was placed in the entrance and Roman soldiers were stationed to guard it from Jesus's disciples.

- We know through other books in the Bible that Jesus descended into hell. He was raised up by the Holy Spirit though, leaving sin in the grave, making a public show of the powers of darkness, and taking away the keys of death and hades.

- Jesus was resurrected on the third day, fulfilling His own prophesy. Though they didn't recognize Him at first, He revealed Himself to His disciples and gave them instructions on moving forward. Jesus was also revealed to a few hundred people and continued to teach on the subject of His kingdom for 40 more days before His ascension into Heaven.

- In the end He breathes on His disciples, telling them to receive the Holy Spirit, and giving them the Great Commission, which is to preach the gospel to the world, making disciples, and baptizing them. But He tells them to wait in Jerusalem until the Holy Spirit descends on them. While the disciples are watching, Jesus is raised up into the heavens and disappears out of sight. We know through other scripture that He now sits enthroned next to His Father, forever making intercession for us who believe.

The Continuation of Jesus's Ministry through His Disciples

Next we'll briefly go over the sequence of events as it is known to have taken place after Jesus's ascension:

- At the start of Acts, the apostles (Jesus's disciples who He called apostles which means "sent ones") are praying and waiting to receive the baptism of the Holy Spirit. With a mighty rushing wind, the Holy Spirit comes with flames of fire and the believers begin to speak in other languages. As this happens, they are forever changed and are empowered to carry out their part of Jesus's plan to save the world.

- The early church is formed as the apostles preach. Peter and John minister in Jerusalem and Samaria. Amazing miracles are accompanying the gospel, and you can see how Jesus's disciples learned from Him and are doing the works that He did, as they are empowered by the Holy Spirit. Even other non-apostolic believers like Stephen also display the power of God working through them.

- Christians are being persecuted and told not to preach in the name of Jesus, but the Holy Spirit continues to fill them and give them boldness.

- A man named Saul who was trained as a Pharisee is one who is persecuting Christians. As he was traveling one day, a bright light blinds him and Jesus speaks out of the light, asking why he is persecuting Him. Saul becomes a believer and is given the new name of Paul. He becomes one of the most prolific writers and ministers of the gospel.

- God shows that His salvation is not only for the Jewish as both Samaritans (half-Jewish people) and Gentiles (non-Jewish people) are becoming believers and being transformed by the infilling of the Holy Spirit. There continue to be persecutions, imprisonments, and miraculous releases in the book of Acts, but despite the persecution the church grows.

- Meanwhile the synoptic gospels are being written (Matthew, Mark, and Luke). They are being referred to as scripture and inspired by the Holy Spirit. The book of James is also probably being written at this time. This is authored by James, not the original disciple, but Jesus's younger brother from His earthly parents, Joseph and Mary.

- Paul and others continue to preach and establish churches all over Asia Minor and Greece. Several of Paul's letters in the New Testament, are written to these churches or other groups of believers that he plans to visit.

- Although it is prophesied that Paul will be imprisoned in Jerusalem if he goes, he feels he needs to minister there. He does end up being imprisoned and goes to trial where he fearlessly proclaims the gospel. As a Roman citizen he is able to appeal to Rome, which he also wanted to travel to for the gospel.

- On the way to Rome, Paul, his jailers, and other prisoners are shipwrecked on an island called Malta. They survive though by listening to Paul's instructions that he received by prayer. On the island Paul ministers in miraculous ways and they have favor with the people there.

- Paul ends up spending the rest of his life imprisoned in Rome and is later beheaded by the Roman Emperor, Nero. But before that he and Peter complete their letters which are included in the Bible. These letters have many keys to living out the life of Christ and explain much of the mysterious aspects of the Bible.

- Lastly, history records that John is almost martyred by being boiled in oil, but survives. He writes the Gospel of John, then 1st, 2nd, and 3rd John. At some point he is exiled to an island called Patmos, where he has the vision recorded in the book of Revelation, and he writes it down.

- Revelation shows so many things, but most importantly that Jesus is Lord and His plans to redeem mankind will be fulfilled. It speaks of the last days, which there are many various interpretations of. Some of it is clear. However, no one knows when it will happen, but the

Antichrist will rise up as a leader who first brings peace, but then demands to be worshiped, and there will be a time of great trials and tribulation. Jesus will then return to the world and eradicate the enemy. God will make a new Heaven and a new Earth. And the faithful will live with Him forever in paradise.

Just like Jesus's disciples follow in His footsteps, we are to also. We continue to be in the last days, and we do not know the day or the hour of Jesus's return. It is said that He will come like a thief in the night. Until that time, we have an opportunity to continue His work of preaching the good news to the whole world, making and baptizing disciples, and allowing God to work miracles through us as we step out in faith.

Prayer

Jesus, You are absolutely wonderful! Thank You for coming to the earth as a man, putting aside for a time Your omnipotence, omniscience, and omnipresence to show us how to live. Thank You for being anointed with power by the Holy Spirit, preaching the good news and destroying the works of the devil, healing all who were oppressed of him

(Acts 10:38). Please help me to walk in these footsteps You exhibited so well. Help me to be filled over and over with the Holy Spirit, that the fruit of the Spirit would be evident in my life, and that the gifts of Your Spirit would help me, just as Your disciples were empowered to live a supernatural life. It is all for Your glory, and that the lost would come to know You, and Your plans would come to pass. I pray this in Your Holy name, Jesus. Hallelujah! Amen!

Chapter 9

The Power of Praise and His Presence

God, keep us near Your
mercy-fountain and bless us!
And when You look down on us,
may Your face beam with joy!
Pause in His presence
Send us out all over the world so that
everyone everywhere
will discover Your ways and
know who You are
and see Your power to save.
Let all the nations burst forth
with praise;

Becoming Supernatural

> *let everyone everywhere love and*
> *enjoy You!*
> *Then how glad the nations will be*
> *when You are their King.*
> *They will sing, they will shout, for*
> *You give true justice to the people.*
> Psalm 67:1-4a TPT

WE'VE DISCUSSED MEETING WITH Jesus and talking with Him. And we've discussed the value of God's Word, even praying it to Him. But we also need to talk about worship and praise, and what it means to press into God. These things happen during prayer, and even the reading of the Bible, but when we specifically focus on praise and worship, and what we'll call pressing into God—something amazing happens. God shows up in profound and life-changing ways.

> *But You are holy,* ***Enthroned in the praises*** *of Israel. Our fathers trusted in You; They trusted, and You delivered them. They cried to You, and were delivered; They trusted in You, and were not ashamed.*
> Psalm 22:2-5 NKJV
> (emphasis added)

Theologically we know that God's presence is everywhere, and the Holy Spirit never leaves us or forsakes us (Acts 17:27-28, Psalm 46:1-2, Psalm 139:7-8, John 14:16-17). But God's manifest presence is something different than His omnipresence. It's when He is acting on our behalf in a tangible way, empowering change. It's when we become aware of His presence because something happened. Whether that awareness manifests as simply a sense of awe, goosebumps, or our hair raising, we know, God is here! Or if it's more obvious and profound, like a physical healing, or the spiritual bursting into the natural, we suddenly become aware of the presence of the Living God—and He blesses us.

May the nations praise you, O God.
Yes, may all the nations praise you.
Then the earth will yield its harvests,
and God, our God, will richly bless us.
Yes, God will bless us,
and people all over the world will fear him.
Psalm 67:5-7 NLT

What Praise and Worship Really Is

If you've spent much time in church you might already have a picture in your mind of what praise and worship is. You might see a band on stage, leading the congregation in songs to God. This definitely can be a wonderful aspect of praise and worship. But it's actually the focus on God, telling Him how much you love Him, honoring Him with your words, and the heart within these activities that matter. Let's not get into semantics of the difference in meaning behind the words praise and worship, but boil things down to what we really need to know and have in our heart.

The enemy would have us think that our worship is doing the things we learn and see other people do in churches, synagogues, mosques, and temples. It's true that we can learn methods from other Christian believers that are helpful. But as we act out or perform a method, it is a slippery slope of becoming dead religion. If we continue in whatever we have learned to do or pray, without truly connecting with God, we are becoming like the Pharisees of the Bible. So let's break down some of the key elements of true worship.

First, we are giving God attention. It isn't about us, our comfort, desires, or what we can get. Although we are thankful for His blessing that comes to us, it's not the reason we praise God. We focus on Him because we recognize He is a person who loves and desires to be loved. We focus on Him because we value and appreciate Him and who He is. We focus on Him to recognize His goodness and thank Him for what He has done.

Secondly, we are expressing our worship to God. Yes,

this is done through raising our hands, playing music to Him, clapping, jumping, and dancing before Him; but our words are a very important part. A husband and wife may really value their loved one looking at them and spending time with them, but if they never hear their spouse use words to share their love, they're going to feel a void. I desire to hear my wife tell me that she loves me, and every once in a while hear her approval of me and positive words about who I am and what I have done. Even so God enjoys it when we use our words to express our love and appreciation of Him.

Lastly, the heart of worship is probably the most important part. We're all put off by disingenuous people. God also doesn't want us to come to Him with empty words and actions without proper motivation. They may fool other people, and even ourselves, but He looks at our hearts (Psalm 51:16-17, Joel 2:13, Provers 16:2, & 1 Samuel 16:7). As we seek His presence, focusing on Him, and speak or sing to Him, He wants to feel the connection of our heart in it. On another note, the heart of worship can be carried into all sorts of things, even work (Colossians 3:23), so whatever you do, let it be praise unto the Lord!

These are the three things I want to bring out, even though I am sure there are more elements we could focus on. Also, I want you to know that in a later book we'll discuss the church, the gathering of believers, the bride of

Christ. We'll talk about how and why we should gather together and the importance of corporate worship. It is a wonderful, beautiful, and powerful thing if done right. In that we will likely reference the verse below again, but here I want our focus to be on our own hearts and private times of worship. This will help us be a valuable addition within the local church body.

> "See then that you walk circumspectly, not as fools but as wise, redeeming the time, because the days are evil. Therefore do not be unwise, but understand what the will of the Lord is. And do not be drunk with wine, in which is dissipation; but be filled with the Spirit, speaking to one another in psalms and hymns and spiritual songs, singing and making melody in your heart to the Lord, giving thanks always for all things to God the Father in the name of our Lord Jesus Christ, submitting to one another in the fear of God."
> Ephesians 5:15-21 NKJV

Press Into God

Armed with the knowledge above, we need to press into God. What I mean by pressing into God, is to seek Him intentionally, even striving with our whole being to enter into His presence and engage with Him. Sometimes this will be for an extended period of time in one sitting, or it can be a heartfelt yearning that lasts for months. Whatever it looks like, there are several scriptures which promise us that we will find God when we seek Him with all our heart (Deuteronomy 4:29, Jeremiah 29:11-13, Matthew 6:6, Hebrews 11:6).

We can know about Jesus, and even have a regular discipline of praying and reading the Bible, but we've got to go deeper. It's the difference between sitting in a room not watching the television, but being aware that a documentary about a lion is on. And grabbing on to the Lion of the Tribe of Judah's mane, pushing your face into that long, soft fur, feeling the purr deep in His chest as you sing out the worship in your heart—and suddenly that Lion tackles you with His strong arms, and licks you in the face!

I have had many times where I prayed and felt nothing. But when I have sought the Lord with a true heart of worship, leaning every part of me into Him, and continued with a zeal and passion that says, "I'm not leaving until You show up!" That's when something incredible happens. That's when my heart touches the Father's, and everything changes. That's when God, our God, appears and richly blesses me (Psalm 67:6).

So in the secret place, wait on the Lord, not inactively in a way that puts you to sleep. But focusing intently on the

Father's face, singing words from all your heart, soul, understanding, and in the mysterious language of the spirit. Tell Jesus how much you love Him and desire to commune with Him. Grab onto the hem of His robe and don't let go. If you continue in these things, whether His response is felt initially or not, you will be blessed. His face will shine upon you. And one day He is going to show up.

Prayer

Oh Lord, deepen my true heartfelt worship of You. I'm thankful for all the methods and prayers I've learned, but I know I need to go deeper. I desire to meet with You and give You the praise that You deserve. Help me to not only seek Your hand of blessing, but to seek Your face. I pray that You would meet with me and show me Your glory. Most of all, that we would commune in a tangible and life-changing way. I will meet with You in the secret place, and sing songs of my love to You and of Your everlasting goodness, and wait for Your presence to overwhelm me. In Jesus's name I pray. Amen!

Chapter 10

Practically Applying the Word

Every Scripture is God-breathed (given by His inspiration) and profitable for instruction, for reproof and conviction of sin, for correction of error and discipline in obedience, [and] for training in righteousness (in holy living, in conformity to God's will in thought, purpose, and action), So that the man of God may be complete and proficient, well fitted and thoroughly equipped for every good work.
2 Timothy 3:16-17 AMPC

WE'RE BRINGING BACK the verses above that I referenced in the Introduction because they are so key to becoming supernatural. Read 2 Timothy 3:16-17 again slowly, and picture how each listed benefit of scripture will help you powerfully live the life God created you to live. We've talked about the Bible quite a lot—appreciating it as the Word of God, reading it daily as nourishment, grasping the big picture, even being transformed to look like Jesus through the Word. There are a few more keys that will help you as you do these things:

- Discerning what scripture is really telling you, and knowing what you should do in response

- Memorizing and meditating on the Bible to have it in your heart

- Allowing God's Word to go from your soul into your spirit

Understanding The Word for Application

My life was literally transformed (again) when I took a certain passage of the Bible and applied it. You'll have to get the next book to learn what that part of scripture was! I'm really not intending to be "click-baity," but that specific passage is not the focus right now. My point is, there are so many verses of the Bible that we read, and maybe even quote, thinking about how good they sound. But have we applied them? Have we slowed down to discern what those verses are really telling us, and perhaps more importantly, are we doing what they say?

It's not a complex, hard, or abstract thing to do. If you break down verses into small components and ask yourself some simple questions, you will be able to do this, which will help you get so much more out of the Bible. And you will understand what to do with what you are reading. Here are those questions:

- What does this tell me about God?
- What does this tell me about the enemy?
- What does this tell me about humanity?
- What does this tell me to do or not do?

Too simple, right? I promise putting it into practice helps more than you might think. Now let's try this out with 2 Timothy 3:16-17, in **NASB** this time to spice things up. First, we break it down into bite sized pieces, and then we answer those questions to the best of our ability. Not every question will be able to be answered with every verse, but we should simply see what the Bible is telling us about these things.

"All Scripture is inspired by God..." God breathed out every verse of the Bible into the writers, therefore I should value each scripture as coming from God.

"... and beneficial for teaching, for rebuke, for correction, for training in righteousness..." God intended the Bible to teach me, rebuke me, correct me, and train me in righteousness. So, I should look for these things within scripture with expectation, submitting to the Word and allowing it to help me learn, tell me where I am wrong, set me straight, and give me the skills needed to live righteously.

"... so that the man or woman of God may be fully capable, equipped for every good work." God will use these things above, so that I, identified as a man of God, am completely able to do the good things He wants me to do, and I have everything that I need to do these good things. This means, I should live as a man of God, believing that through His Word God has made me able and given me all I need to do good works.

Imagine what amazing things would happen if you kept this passage in mind and put the things it's telling you to do into practice!

John W. Nichols

Memorizing and Meditating on Scripture

Blessed is the man Who walks not in the counsel of the ungodly, Nor stands in the path of sinners, Nor sits in the seat of the scornful; But his delight is in the law of the Lord, And in His law he meditates day and night. He shall be like a tree Planted by the rivers of water, That brings forth its fruit in its season, Whose leaf also shall not wither; And whatever he does shall prosper.
Psalms 1:1-3 NKJV

The Bible is often referred to as the law because of God dictating the law to Moses, who wrote it down verbatim, and it is part of the first five books of scripture. Because all scripture is God-breathed, verses which speak of "the law," can often be applied to all of the Bible. This means that the opening of Psalms tells us to meditate on the Word, and how we will be blessed and prosperous as we do.

Don't worry, we aren't heading in a New Age direction, this meditation is not an emptying of your mind so the demonic can have their way. But a filling of your mind with scripture. You will take a passage and continue to focus on it, allowing it to go deep within you, knowing it more profoundly. And you will receive revelation and wisdom from the Holy Spirit to both understand and apply what you meditate on.

This time let's take the passage we just referenced above, Psalm 1:1-3, and follow these instructions:

- In a quiet place where you can focus and give God your devotion, continue to read these verses (or a portion of them) over and over, while asking the Holy Spirit to speak in your heart.

- Each time you read the passage, emphasize and focus on the next individual key-word, considering its meaning, and what it adds to the passage. This means as many meaningful words as are in the passage, will be at least the number of times you go over it in meditation.

- Picture yourself in the verse, doing the good things it says to do, or in the position of a person in the passage that is obeying God. This can actually take you into a profound spiritual experience of that Word.

As you do these things, you will not only understand the passage you are meditating on much better, and know how to practically apply it, but you will be transformed by it. This is also a great way to memorize scripture. Because you are going over it again and again, focusing on each word, your mind is being renewed and the seed of God's word is being planted in your heart.

Even if you use a different method for memorizing

scripture, like speaking it aloud over and over with the passage in front of you, and then trying to speak it without looking at the passage (or any other preferred method of memorization), you will be blessed as you show God how you value His Word. Memorizing and meditating on scripture allows it to be available to you any time during the day or night. You will find the Holy Spirit reminds you of these passages, you will take steps in living them out, and you will speak them into the circumstances and lives of people around you.

The Seed of God's Word Taking Deeper Roots

> *The seed that fell on good soil represents those who truly hear and understand God's word and produce a harvest of thirty, sixty, or even a hundred times as much as had been planted!*
> Matthew 13:23 NLT

In Matthew 13 Jesus tells a parable about a farmer sowing seed and then explained to His disciples what it meant. The seed of God's word being planted in your heart is a real and invaluable occurrence. As you do the things we are talking about in this chapter, that seed is taking root in you, and going deeper than the soul-level. And it is able to reproduce, not only in your life, but in the lives of people around you.

Remember, in Chapter 4, we talked about how the Word is sharp and able to divide between soul and spirit? And how our soul is a part of us that operates in many ways, including the use of our natural understanding and knowledge? We need the Word of God's roots to penetrate deeper than the soul-level, because it produces wisdom, revelation, and faith. Living based off these Holy Spirit imparted gifts, will take us so much further than living based on head-knowledge.

When we have Godly wisdom, we will better know how to apply the Word. When the Holy Spirit brings revelation, we see these passages in a new and living light. When we have faith, we allow the scriptures to take us places we wouldn't dream of. All these things help us reflect Jesus supernaturally. And that's what this has all been about!

Prayer

Jesus, the Word of God made flesh, help me practice these tools for greater understanding, application, memorization, and meditation on Your precious scriptures. I want to receive a deeper understanding of You, our enemy, humanity, and what I should do with Your

Word. Holy Spirit, please empower me to meditate on Bible passages and receive Your impartation. Father, sow the seed of Your Word, deep into my heart and help it to grow roots. I want to go deeper than head-knowledge into the realm of supernatural revelation, wisdom, and faith. Thank You, Lord. In Jesus's name I pray. Amen!

Chapter 11

Following the Spirit of Truth

YOU PROBABLY HAVE THOUGHT about how wonderful it would be to have Jesus by your side all the time. I definitely have thought that, and so did Jesus's disciples moments before He went to the cross. Even though He came in to Jerusalem practically being worshiped as a Savior King, He had told His disciples that He would be going to His Father. But they still didn't really get it. Then He said, "Now I am going away to the one who sent me, and not one of you is asking where I am going. Instead, you grieve because of what I've told you. But in fact, *it is best for you that I go away*, because if I don't, the Advocate won't come. If I do go away, then I will send Him to you. (John 16:5-7 NLT emphasis added)."

Peter's transformation we talked about in the chapter on the baptism of the Holy Spirit, couldn't have happened if Jesus stayed with His disciples. It is literally best for us that He went, so that He could send His Spirit. But notice something He says about the Holy Spirit a few verses later.

> *"When He, the Spirit of truth, comes, He will guide you into all the truth; for He will not speak on His own, but whatever He hears, He will speak; and He will disclose to you what is to come. He will glorify Me, for He will take from Mine and will disclose it to you. All things that the Father has are Mine; this is why I said that He takes from Mine and will disclose it to you."*
> John 16:13-15 NASB

In both the last book and this one, we have highlighted the fact that Jesus didn't do anything on His own initiative (John 8:28-30, John 14:10-14). Both His words and works were led by the Father. I find it amazing that He's saying something similar about the Holy Spirit of truth. He also will not speak on His own! Everything of the Father's has been shared with Jesus, and through the working of the Holy Spirit in submission to the Father, we become partakers of this inheritance.

If both Jesus and the Holy Spirit are not acting on their own accord. Then how much more are our lives not our own? We must strip ourselves of any independence from God. Jesus was dependent on the Father, the Holy Spirit is dependent on Jesus, and we must be dependent on the Holy Spirit. We simply aren't meant to do and say whatever we want, but we're supposed to follow our Heavenly Father, through the leading of the Holy Spirit within us.

> *For those who live according to the flesh set their minds on the things of the flesh, but those who live according to the Spirit, the things of the Spirit. For to be carnally minded is death, but to be spiritually minded is life and peace. Because the carnal mind is enmity against God; for it is not subject to the law of God, nor indeed can be. So then, those who are in the flesh cannot please God.*
> *But you are not in the flesh but in the Spirit, if indeed the Spirit of God dwells in you.*
> Romans 8:5-9a NKJV
> (see also Galatians 5:13-26)

Living Out the Truth in the Power of the Holy Spirit

As we've looked at overviews of the living pages of the

Old and New Testaments, we've seen what has led up to this amazing time to be alive. It would do us good to consider it again, recognizing how the Holy Spirit empowers us to live the life which scripture equips us for. We've seen that there is a loving and all-powerful Creator who made everything, including what we can see and what we can't. His Spirit was intimately involved in it all, and continues to be. But out of love and the desire for free devotion, He gives enough room and mystery for His ultimate power to not subdue and control everything. (Genesis 1:1-2, Hebrews 11:3, Romans 2:4, 2 Peter 1:3-18)

We've also seen that God has made many types of beings who exercise quite a bit of free will, in a seemingly autonomous way. This includes heavenly and earthly creatures, various kinds of angelic beings, and only one creation said to be made in His image—humanity. The Bible has shown us glimpses revealing both heavenly and natural realms are inhabited by beings which God has given responsibilities. Of these, His Spirit has chosen to dwell within mankind. (Genesis 1:26-28, Job 1:6 & 2:1, 1 Kings 22:19-23, Ezekiel 28:13-14, Psalm 8:3-6, Psalm 89:5-8, Daniel 7:9-10, Ezekiel 1:4-28, Nehemiah 9:6, Revelation 4:6-11)

Certain angelic beings were given areas of authority including principalities and other entrusted charges to watch over. Remember the Bible shows that a large number of these angelic beings have fallen away from God at some point in history. This includes ones over regions of the earth, who secretly continue desiring to be worshipped as gods. Although we can't see them in the natural, they are no less real, so we need the Holy Spirit's discernment. (Daniel 10:12-13, Ezekial 28:13-19, Ephesians 3:10-11, Ephesians 6:11-12, Colossians 1:16, Jude 1:6, Revelation 12:1-17, Revelation 17:1-18)

In order to deceive and control the world, the enemy has taken advantage of these spiritual mysteries, God's apparent absence, and His allowance of autonomy in His creation. This deception has led humanity to give rulership of the world to the fallen beings that God didn't intend to have control. This has also resulted in corruption of flesh, worship of false-gods, and demonic entities. But we have seen how God always had a plan that was greater. (Genesis 3:1-19, Genesis 6:1-13, Genesis 10:8-10 & 11:1-9, Leviticus 17:7, Deuteronomy 12:29-31, Psalm 106:34-48, Luke 8:26-39, Romans 1:22-23, Revelation 12:9, 1 John 5:19, Ephesians 2:1-2, 2 Corinthians 4:4)

When we look back to humanity's beginning, we see we were created as good and in God's image. However, the first man, Adam, chose to sin. Through this a sinful nature came into the world and passed to all humanity. God gave humanity dominion over the earth, so He also needed to redeem mankind through a human, but none were righteous. The many prophesies throughout scripture about a Savior, show that God is masterfully working in and around us to bring redemption. Jesus fulfilled these prophecies. God used a part of humanity's blood-line, and by His Spirit, places His only begotten Son in it, born of a virgin. Through His perfect sinless life, and when He took the sins of the world during His death and in His powerful resurrection, He conquered sin and death and brought mankind back into his destiny. (Romans 3:10, Romans 5:12-21, Genesis 3:15, Jeremiah 23:5, Isaiah 7:14-16, Isaiah 9:7, Isaiah 53:1-12, Matthew 1:1-16, Luke 1:26-38, Luke 3:21-38, John 3:16-18, Galatians 4:4-7, Hebrews 2:8-18, Revelation 13:8, Revelation 5:5-14, Ephesians 1:7-14)

Now we are in the end times, and this Savior has given us His mighty Holy Spirit, power, and authority over the enemy. All of this has led up to this moment in history, where God will increase His glory and Lordship over the earth through you and me, as we are led by His Spirit, as we preach the gospel, and He ultimately redeems the heavens and the earth. It's an amazing time to live and to be a follower of Jesus, filled with the Holy Spirit! (Luke 10:17-20, Matthew 24:13-14, Mark 16:15-18, Acts 2:17-21, Romans 8:18-30, Romans 16:20, Hebrews 2:10, 1 Corinthians 15:20-28, 2 Corinthians 5:17-21, Ephesians 1:15-23, Revelation 12:11, Revelation 21-22).

Trading the Natural Life for the Spiritual

> *We crave for all that is mortal to be swallowed up by eternal life. And this is no empty hope, for God Himself is the one who has prepared us for this wonderful destiny. And to confirm this promise, He has given us the Holy Spirit, like an engagement ring, as a guarantee.*
>
> *That's why we're always full of courage. Even while we're at home in the body, we're homesick to be with the Master—for we live by faith, not by what we see with our eyes.*
>
> 2 Corinthians 5:4b-7 TPT
> (see also 2 Corinthians 4:18)

God is calling you to look at life from His supernatural perspective. He created us not only as physical beings, but spiritual. And though there is a deep and dark deception which has even led us astray many times, He's given you the Holy Spirit of truth. This Spirit of the Living God will help you discern spiritual things and gift you with the ability to live a life pleasing to your Creator. It's not about being perfect, but being perfected through obedience.

> *It was fitting for Him, for whom are all things, and through whom are all things, in bringing many sons to glory, to perfect the originator*

> *of their salvation through sufferings. For both He who sanctifies and those who are sanctified are all from one Father; for this reason He is not ashamed to call them brothers and sisters.*
> Hebrews 1:10-11 NASB

Jesus's literal death-to-self has given you this life you are living. The Bible says, "You do not belong to yourself, for God bought you with a high price. So you must honor God with your body (1 Corinthians 6:19a-20 NLT)." This living not by the flesh but by the Spirit, is why Jesus is not ashamed to be called your older brother and to share His inheritance with you.

Jesus and the Holy Spirit both model for us a letting go of control. In the garden, as He was dealing with the idea that this great cup of suffering was coming fast upon Him, Jesus said to the Father, "Not my will but Yours be done (Luke 22:42)." Even as He tells you to take up your cross and follow Him, He gives a hope that He will somehow lighten this burden of giving up your life.

> *"Come to me, all of you who are weary and carry heavy burdens, and I will give you rest. Take my yoke upon you. Let me teach you, because I am humble and gentle at heart, and you will find rest for your souls. For my yoke is easy to bear, and the burden I give you is*

light."
Matthew 11:28 NLT

No matter the cost, this burden of Jesus is light, because it is a removal of being your own god. You can let go of trying to plan and make everything work. You can let go of figuring it out. You can let go of your obligation to fix it all and be the hero. It all comes down to one responsibility, walking in fellowship with God, as His child. If you take care of this one thing, everything else will fall into place.

Being Led by the Spirit

Remember Jesus said:

"The hour is coming, and now is, when the true worshipers will worship the Father in spirit and truth; for the Father is seeking such to worship Him. God is Spirit, and those who worship Him must worship in spirit and truth."
John 4:23-24 NKJV

Shortly after these words, Jesus's disciples were trying to get Him to eat. But He said, "My food is to do the will of Him who sent Me, and to finish His work (v.34)." Sustenance comes through giving up the leading of the flesh and submitting to the Father in spirit and truth. As we live a supernatural life of true worship (Romans 12:1-2), our natural life is taken care of (Matthew 6:25-34).

Just as Jesus sent His disciples in Matthew 10, He is sending you. He is giving you "authority over unclean spirits, to cast them out, and to heal every disease and every sickness (v.1)." And He's instructing you "As you go, preach, saying, 'The kingdom of heaven has come near.' Heal the sick, raise the dead, cleanse those with leprosy, cast out demons. Freely you received, freely give (v.8)."

He tells you how to handle the persecution that will come, saying, "Do not worry about how or what you are to say; for what you are to say will be given you in that hour. For it is not you who are speaking, but it is the Spirit of your Father who is speaking in you (v.19-20). A disciple is not above his teacher, nor a slave above his master. It is enough for the disciple that he may become like his teacher, and the slave like his master. If they have called the head of the house Beelzebul, how much more will they insult the members of his household (v.24-25)!"

It reminds me of how the Holy Spirit doesn't speak on His own accord, and how He leads us into all truth, as Jesus continues, "Do not fear them, for there is nothing concealed that will not be revealed, or hidden that will not be known. What I tell you in the darkness, tell in the light; and what you hear whispered in your ear, proclaim on the housetops (v.26-27)."

You see, as the Son has glorified the Father who sent Him, the Father has also glorified the Son. Now the One who gave up His life is sending you, saying, "The one who does not take his cross and follow after Me is not worthy of Me. The one who has found his life will lose it, and the one who has lost his life on My account will find it. The one who receives you receives Me, and the one who receives Me receives Him who sent Me (v.38-40)."

As you respond to these words of Jesus in faith, you will lay down your life and walk in step with Him, following His Spirit. Though you may fail at times, and you are definitely not God in the flesh, you will be able to copy Jesus saying, "The words that I say to you I do not speak on my own, but the Father, as He remains in me, does His works. Believe me that I am in the Father and the Father is in me; otherwise believe because of the works themselves (John 14:10b-11 NASB)."

The Holy Spirit is empowering you to walk this out, in spirit and in truth, so that you are supernatural.

Prayer

Holy Spirit, thank You for filling me and leading me into all truth. Thank You for showing me how to live in obedience to the Father, just as Jesus showed as well. This world, the enemy, and my flesh are vying for my affections, but what they offer is nothing compared to the life You have for me. I declare that I desire to live and walk by the Spirit, and not by the flesh. You've placed me here, in this time, for a specific reason. And I don't want to waste this opportunity to be used by You. So I will take up my cross daily, listening and obeying, and being perfected in relationship with You. I give up this short natural life, so that I can gain true everlasting life. Please help me to put all this into practice. I want to follow in Jesus's footsteps, worshiping in spirit and truth, and being sustained as I do My Heavenly Father's supernatural work. Thank You, Lord, amen!

Additional Notes

I HOPE MY WORDS have blessed you and encouraged you to step into the calling you have in Christ. If they have, there are a few ways you can be even more blessed, forward the blessing to someone else, and help me at the same time. Check out all the free stuff I have for you below and find out how to partner with me and my family.

Who Needs to Hear this Message?

Take a moment and ask God to show you who else this book or series could help. He may bring someone to your mind that you want to be inspired to change the world. Or maybe someone who needs a deeper revelation of the Holy Spirit, the Bible, and worshiping in spirit and in truth. This book and the other books in the series would also be good for Bible study material.

If you or someone you know is fighting for physical healing or would like to learn more about how to pray for healing, you should check out my book, *Healing is Here*. It is a 7-week devotional that shows God's will to heal and how to pray for it using Biblical examples. Find out more

Becoming Supernatural

at:

GodAndYouAndMe.com/Healing-is-Here-Book

If you know someone who is going through a hard time, or struggling with questions about life and God, you can let them know they can get my ebook *GOD is HERE*, the accompanying workbook and journal, audiobook, and PDF on salvation and the gift of the Holy Spirit for free here:

GodAndYouAndMe.com/God-is-Here-Free-Stuff

Reviews are a Huge Help to Authors

Another way to help is with a few minutes of your time by leaving a quick review wherever you got this book. Reviews really help people to know if they should check out a book. You can review it on Amazon, Good Reads, Barnes & Noble, iBooks, Kobo, and/or Google Play Books. Please take a couple of minutes to review this book on one or more of these sites. I appreciate your feedback, so I can learn to communicate God's heart better, and hopefully reach more people. Thank you in advance!

More Free Books!

If you're interested in being an advance reader and have the opportunity to get future books for free, visit:

GodAndYouAndMe.com/Advance-Reader

Updates and Partnering with My Family

If you'd like an update on what God is doing with me and my family, and would like to support us in prayer or financially visit:

GodAndYouAndMe.com/Ministry-Partner

My Contact Information

Check out the About the Author chapter below for a bit more info about me and my family, as well as how you can contact me, connect on social media, and receive encouraging blog posts on my website. I would love to hear any testimonies of the work that God has done in your life through my work. Please reach out below.

Free Stuff!

IF YOU HAVEN'T ALREADY, be sure to download the free resources I've made available!

Subscribe at: GodAndYouAndMe.com/becoming-supernatural-free-stuff

Get These Free Resources Together

- *God is Trying to Tell You Something.* An audio teaching in MP3 format, focused on the key to hearing God, common ways God speaks, and practical steps to hear Him today.

- *7 Keys to a Successful Time of Devotion to God.* A PDF with steps to include in your quiet time.
- *Navigating the Maze of Life with God.* A 60-page PDF about giving your life to God, being filled with the Holy Spirit, and walking in the power of the Holy Spirit to live the life God intended you to live.
- Additional content only available to subscribers on GodAndYouAndMe.com. You can unsubscribe at any time and I promise not to spam you.

Get these free resources here (Most phones are capable of using the camera app to follow this link. Simply open the camera on your phone and point it at the page):

GodAndYouAndMe.com/becoming-supernatural-free-stuff

About the Author

JESUS RADICALLY SAVED John W. Nichols at the age of twenty. As a child he had loved to read and write, but drugs and alcohol had stolen his identity. Through the prayers and lives of a few people, he had a revelation of the love of God, and started reading His great love letter, the Holy Bible. As John laid everything down at Jesus's feet, his life was never the same.

He so wanted to serve the Lord, and give Him every talent. He thought one day (when he was old) he might write a book for God. But God thought he should write something sooner, and told John in a prayer session on January 1st, 2016, to write his book. Since then, John has written five books including the one you are reading.

In other prayer sessions, God called John to preach His Word, seek His face, and go into the land He would show Him. He and his wife, Trinna, and their three children, are following this call to show the love of Christ to the world. This was first exhibited teaching and leading worship in their local church, then by working with people with disabilities, then going to preach at the state prison, loving their neighborhood community, reaching out to women and children enslaved in human trafficking, making disciples of Jesus who will multiply, and now serving as missionaries in Rome, Italy.

When John caught a glimpse of how God saw him, everything changed, and he has since sought to show others this good news. He's recognized most people, Christian or not, feel unfulfilled and don't know their life's purpose. This has led John to help people find their calling and have a life of adventure with God. To be encouraged in the way God sees you, and to keep up with what God is doing with John and his family, go to:

You can also connect with John in the following ways.
Email:
John@GodAndYouAndMe.com
Short words of encouragement:
GodAndYouAndMe.com/Blog

Social Media:
Facebook.com/GodAndYouAndMeBlog
YouTube.com/channel/UCqG-TKZgn2PwwEQx9WlThoA
Istagram.com/Nichols_JohnW
Twitter.com/Nichols_JohnW

Linkedin.com/in/GodAndYouAndMe
GoodReads.com/author/show/18325435.John_W_Nichols
Amazon.com/author/Nichols_JohnW

www.ingramcontent.com/pod-product-compliance
Lightning Source LLC
Chambersburg PA
CBHW060607080526
44585CB00013B/722